Richard Hooper, George Sandys

Poetical Works

Vol. 2

Richard Hooper, George Sandys

Poetical Works

Vol. 2

ISBN/EAN: 9783337217501

Printed in Europe, USA, Canada, Australia, Japan

Cover: Foto ©Thomas Meinert / pixelio.de

More available books at **www.hansebooks.com**

Library of Old Authors.

THE POETICAL WORKS OF
GEORGE SANDYS.

NOW FIRST COLLECTED.

WITH INTRODUCTION AND NOTES BY

THE REV. RICHARD HOOPER, M.A.
VICAR OF UPTON AND ASTON UPTHORPE, BERKS,
AND EDITOR OF CHAPMAN'S HOMER.

VOLUME II.

LONDON:
JOHN RUSSELL SMITH,
SOHO SQUARE.
1872.

CHISWICK PRESS:—PRINTED BY WHITTINGHAM AND WILKINS,
TOOKS COURT, CHANCERY LANE.

A PARAPHRASE
UPON THE THIRD BOOK OF THE
PSALMS OF DAVID.

A PARAPHRASE
UPON THE THIRD BOOK OF THE PSALMS OF DAVID.

PSALM LXXIII.

PART I.   *Tune 1.*

THAT Pow'r of pow'rs, who Israel protects,
The pure of heart eternally affects.
Yet I began to stagger in my faith,
My feet almost had swervéd from His path,
When I the fool beheld with envious eyes,
Saw prosp'rous vice to wealth and honour rise.
Their thread of life is close and firmly spun,
Whom feeble age and pale diseases shun.
They, while we suffer, surfeit in content,
As if alone exempt from punishment.
Pride hangs like precious chains about their necks,
And violence in robes of purple decks.
Their swoll'n eyes shine with uncontroll'd excess,
Who more than what their hearts can wish possess,
Ev'n glory in their foul impiety,
And speak like thunder from the troubled sky.
Dire blasphemies against high Heav'n they cast,
The suff'ring earth their pride and slander blast.

The good not seldom through their scandal stray,
And, press'd with miseries, in passion say:
O how can we the Lord All-seeing call,
Or think He cares what unto men befall,
When lo! the wicked with success are crown'd,
And in the pleasures of this world abound?
I to no end have purg'd my heart of stain,
In innocence have cleans'd my hands in vain,
That thus with daily punishments am worn,
And still chastiséd with the rising morn.

PART II:

If I gave words unto such thoughts as these,
I should th' assemblies of Thy saints displease;
For then what were it to be just or good?
My soul this secret never understood,
Till I into Thy sanctuary came,
And there beheld their honour end in shame.
Thou hast on slipp'ry heights their greatness plac'd,
Down headlong from their noon of glory cast.
How are they unto desolation brought,
Consuméd in the moment of a thought!
Such as a pleasant dream when sleep forsakes
Our flatter'd sense; so, when Thy wrath awakes,
Thou in Thy dreadful fury shalt destroy
Their empty and imaginary joy.
These former thoughts did my weak soul molest,
So ignorant, so vain, so like a beast.
Yet I by Thy Divine supportance stand,
Thou held'st me up by Thy Almighty Hand.
Thou by Thy counsel shalt direct my ways,
And after to eternal glory raise.
For whom have I but Thee in heav'n above?
Or what on earth can my affections move?
My thoughts and flesh are frail; yet, Lord, Thou art
My portion, and the vigour of my heart.

Who Thee abandon shall to death descend,
And they whose knees to cursèd idols bend.
I as my duty will to God repair,
On Him rely and His great acts declare.

PSALM LXXIV.

PART I. *Tune* 12.

LORD, why hast Thou abandonèd?
   O why for ever shall Thine ire
   Consume, like a devouring fire,
The sheep which in Thy pastures fed?

O think of those who were Thy own,
   By Thee of old from bondage brought;
   Th' inheritance which Thou hast bought,
And Sion, Thy affected throne.

Come, O come quickly, and survey
   What spoil the barbarous foe hath made.
   Lo! all in heaps of ruins laid,
Thy temple their accursèd prey.

Like lions, with sharp famine whet,
   They in Thy sanctuary roar;
   All purple in Thy people's gore,
And there their conqu'ring ensigns set.

It was esteem'd a great renown
   With axe to square the mountain oaks;
   Now they demolish with their strokes
And hew the carvèd fabric down.

Who lo! with all-enfolding flame
   The beauty of the earth devour;
   Profanely prostrate on the floor
That temple sacred to Thy Name.

Now (said they) with a sudden hand
  Give we a gen'ral end to all.
  By fire the holy structures fall
Through this depopulated land.

PART II.

No miracles amaze our foes,
  There are no prophets to divine,
  That might our miseries decline,
None know the period of our woes.

Ah! how long shall our enemies
  Exult and glory in our shame!
  How long shall they blaspheme Thy Name,
Great God, and Thy slow wrath despise!

Thy Hand out of Thy bosom draw,
  Nor longer Thy revenge withhold;
  My God, Thou wast our king; the old
Amazéd world Thy wonders saw.

Thou struck'st the Erythræan waves
  When seas from seas in tumult fled;
  Brak'st the Egyptian dragon's head,
And mad'st the joining floods their graves.

That great Leviathan of Nile,
  To beasts and serpents which possess
  The dry and foodless wilderness,
By Thee deliver'd for a spoil.

Thou clav'st the rock, from whose green [1] wound
  The thirst-expelling fountain brake;
  Thou mad'st the heady streams forsake
Their channels, and become dry ground.

---

[1] *Green*, i. e. fresh.

Part III.

The cheerful day, night cloth'd in shade,
  The moon and radiant sun are Thine;
  Thy bounds the swelling seas confine,
Summer and winter by Thee made.

Great God of gods, forget not those
  Who Thee reproachfully despise.
  Remember, Lord, the blasphemies
Cast on Thee by our frantic foes.

O! to the wicked multitude
  Surrender not Thy turtle-dove;
  Nor from Thy tender care remove
The poor, by pow'rful wrong pursu'd.

Thy cov'nant, bound by oath, maintain;
  For darkness overspreads the face
  Of all the land; in ev'ry place
Destruction, rape, and slaughter reign.

Let not th' opprest return with shame,
  But crown Thee with deserv'd applause;
  O patronise Thy proper cause;
Remember, fools revile Thy name.

O let their sorrows never cease
  Who blast Thee with their calumnies.
  The tumults of their pride who rise
Against Thee, ev'ry day increase.

PSALM LXXV.

Tune 7.

THY praises, O eternal King,
  Our souls in sacred verse will sing,
  The wonders of Thy works declare,
Thy presence in Thy pow'r and care.

When I shall wear the Hebrew crown,
High justice shall my reign renown.
The land with weak'ning discord rent,
The people without government,
Faint and dissolve.   Her pillars I
Support, her breaches fortify.
Proud man, I said, renounce thy pride,
Thou fool, thy folly cast aside,
Do not so high your horns erect,
Nor bellow as with yoke uncheck'd.
Preferment from the orient,
Nor from the evening sun's descent,
Nor desert, comes.   God guides our fates,
He raiseth and he ruinates.
A cup of red and mingled wine
He poureth out to me and mine.
But every rebel in the land
Shall drink the dregs, squeez'd by His Hand.
His noble acts I will relate,
The God of Jacob celebrate ;
Suppress the wicked and their ways,
The just to wealth and honour raise.

PSALM LXXVI.

Tune 15.

GOD in Judah is renown'd,
Salem with his temple crown'd.
He in sacred Sion dwells,
Israel His wonders tells.
He their flying ensigns tears,
Shivers the Assyrian spears.
He their swords, shields, arrows, broke;
Kill'd, subdu'd, without a stroke.
Thou more excellent than they
That on Jewry's mountains prey.

Who the great in battle foil'd,
Of their lives and honours spoil'd.
Not the mighty could withstand,
Nor so much as find a hand.
Princes, by Thy only breath,
With the vulgar sleep in death.
Terrible unto Thy foes,
O, who can Thy wrath oppose?
When as they Thy thunder hear,
Mortals stand amaz'd and fear;
When from Thy eternal rest
Thou descend'st to save th' oppress'd.
Malice but itself betrays,
And converts into Thy praise.
Future rage Thou shalt restrain,
Making their endeavours vain.
Jacob's seed, with one accord,
Pay your vows unto the Lord.
Holy Levites, off'rings bring,
Of His glorious conquest sing.
He Who princes overthrows,
O, how fearful to His foes!

PSALM LXXVII.

Tune 5.

PART I.

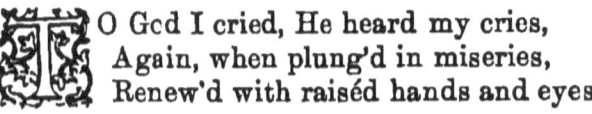O God I cried, He heard my cries,
Again, when plung'd in miseries,
Renew'd with raiséd hands and eyes.

My fester'd wounds ran all the night,
No comfort could my soul invite
To relish long outworn delight.

I call'd upon the Ever-blest,
And yet my troubles still increas'd,
Almost to death by sorrow press'd.

Thou keep'st my gallèd eyes awake;
Words fail my grief; sighs only spake,
Which from my panting bosom brake.

Then did my memory unfold
The wonders which Thou wrought'st of old,
By our admiring fathers told.

The songs which in the night I sung,
When deeply by affliction stung,
These thoughts thus mov'd my desperate tongue:

Wilt Thou for ever, Lord, forsake?
Nor pity on th' afflicted take?
O shall Thy mercy never wake?

Wilt Thou Thy promise falsify?
Must I in Thy displeasure die?
Shall grace before Thy fury fly?

This said, I thus my passions check'd,
His changes on their ends reflect,
To punish and restore th' elect.

PART II.

His great deliverance shall dwell
In my remembrance; I will tell
What in our fathers' days befell.

His counsels from our reach are set,
Hid in His sacred cabinet.
What God like ours, so good, so great?

Who wonders can effect alone,
His people's great redemptión,
To Jacob's seed, and Joseph's known.

The yielding floods confess Thy might,
The deeps were troubled at Thy sight,
And seas recoil'd in their affright.

The clouds in storms of rain descend,
The air thy hideous fragors rend,
Thy arrows dreadful flames extend.

Thy thunders roaring rake the skies,
Thy fatal light'ning swiftly flies,
Earth trembles in her agonies.

Thy ways ev'n through the billows lie,
The floods then left their channels dry,
No mòrtal can Thy steps descry.

Like flocks, through wilderness of sand,
Thou ledd'st us to this pleasant land,
By Moses' and by Aaron's hand.

PSALM LXXVIII.

PART I. *Tune* 18.

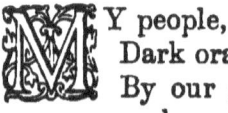Y people, hear my words: I will unfold
Dark oracles and wonders done of old;
By our great ancestors both heard and
    known,
Successively unto their children shown.
Which we will to posterity relate,
That people yet unknown may celebrate
God's pow'r, His praise and glorious acts; since He
Wills this tradition by divine decree,
Until one day shall give the world an end,
That all their hopes might on His help depend.
Nor ever let His noble actions sleep
In dark oblivion, but His statutes keep.

Unlike their rebel sires, a stubborn race,
Who fell from God, nor sought His slighted grace.
The Ephraimites, though expert in their bows,
Though arm'd, ignobly fled before their foes ;
Who vainly brake the cov'nant of their God,
Nor in the ways of His prescription trod;
Forgot His famous acts, His wonders shown
In Zoan, and the plains by Nile o'erflown.
He brought them through the bowels of the flood,
The parted waves like solid mountains stood.
By day with leading clouds affords a shade,
By night a flaming pyramis display'd.
Hard rocks He in the thirsty deserts clave,
And drink out of their stony entrails gave.
Ev'n from their barren sides the waters gush'd,
And down in rivers through the valleys rush'd.

PART II.

Yet still they sinn'd, and meat to satisfy
Their lust demand, provoking the Most High.
Blaspheming thus : Can God our wants redress ?
A table furnish in the wilderness ?
Though from the cloven rocks fresh currents drill,
Can He give bread ? with flesh the hungry fill ?
Thus tempted by their hourly murmurings,
He to His long retarded wrath gives wings.
Their infidelity enrag'd the Just,
That would not to His sure protection trust.
Who all the curtains of the skies withdrew,
And made the clouds resolve into a dew.
With manna, food of angels, mortals fed,
And fill'd with plenty of celestial bread.
Then caus'd the early eastern winds to rise,
And bade the dropping south obscure the skies ;

Whence show'rs of quails descend, as thick as
   sand
On sea-wash'd shores, or dust on sun-dried land,
Which fell among their tents. They their delights
Enjoy, and feast their deadly appetites.
For lo! while they those fatal dainties chew,
And their inordinate desires pursue,
The wrath of God surpris'd them, and cut down
The choice of all, ev'n those of most renown.
Nor by their own mishaps admonishéd,
Would they His work believe or judgments dread.
So He their spirits quench'd with daily fears,
In vanity and toil consum'd their years.

PART III.

But when, by slaughter wasted, the forlorn
Return'd and sought Him in the early morn,
They then confess'd and said: Thou art our tow'r,
Our strength, alone protectest by Thy pow'r.
Yet their sly tongues did but their souls disguise,
Full of deluding flatteries and lies.
Their faithless hearts revolted from His will,
Nor ever would His just commands fulfill.
How oft would He Whose mercy hath no bound
Their pardon sign, nor in their sins confound!
How oft did He His burning wrath assuage!
How oft divert the fury of His rage!
Consider'd them as flesh in frailty born,
A passing wind that never can return.
Yet still would they His sacred laws transgress,
Provok'd Him in th' unpeopled wilderness,
Confin'd the Holy One of Israel,
Against their Saviour frantickly rebell.
Forgetful of His pow'r, nor ever thought
Of that great day when from long bondage brought,

His dreadful miracles to Egypt known,
And wonders in the field of Zoan shown.
The river chang'd into a sea of blood,
Men faint for thirst t' avoid th' infected flood.
Huge swarms of unknown flies display their wings,
Which wound to death with their envenom'd stings.
Loath'd frogs ev'n in their palaces abound,
And with their filthy slime pollute the ground.

PART IV.

Their early fruits the caterpillars spoil,
And grasshoppers devour the ploughman's toil.
Long vines with storms their dangling burdens lost,
The broad-leav'd sycamores destroy'd with frost.
Their flocks, beat down with hailstones, breathless lie,
Their cattle by the stroke of thunder die.
The vengeance of His wrath all forms of woes,
More plagues than could be fear'd, upon them throws;
Whom evil angels to their sins betray.
He to the torrent of His wrath gave way,
Nor would with man or sinless beasts dispense,
Shot by the arrows of his pestilence.
Slew all the flow'r of youth, their first-born sons,
There where old Nilus in seven channels runs.
But like a flock of sheep His people led,
Safe and secure through deserts full of dread;
Ev'n through unfathom'd deeps, which part and close
Their tumbling waves to swallow their proud foes.
Then brought them to His consecrated land,
Ev'n to His mountain purchas'd by His Hand.

Cast out the giant-like inhabitants,
And in their rooms the tribes of Israel plants.
Yet they (O most ungrateful!) falsify
Their vows, and still exasp'rate the Most High,
Who in their faithless fathers' traces go,
And start aside like a deceitful bow.
Their altars on the tops of mountains blaze,
While they their hands to cursed idols raise.

PART V.

These objects fuel to His wrath afford,
Whose Soul revolted Israel abhorr'd.
The ancient seat of Shiloh then forsook,
Nor longer would that hated mansion brook.
His ark ev'n to captivity declin'd,
His strength and glory to the foe resign'd,
And yielded up His people to the rage
Of barbarous swords, nor would His wrath assuage.
Devouring flames their able youth confound,
Nor are their maids with nuptial garlands
 crown'd.
Their mitred priests in heat of battle fall,
No widows weeping at their funeral.
Then as a giant, folded in the charms
Of wine and sleep, starts up and cries, To arms.
So rous'd, His foes behind Jehovah wounds,
And with eternal infamy confounds.
Yet would in Joseph's tents no longer dwell,
Nor Ephraim chose, who from His cov'nant fell;
But Judah's mountain for His seat elects,
And sacred Sion, which He most affects.
There our great God His glorious temple plac'd,
Firm as the centre, never to be raz'd.
And from the bleating flocks His David chose,
When he attended on the yeaning ewes,

And rais'd him to a throne, that he might feed
His people, Israel's selected seed.
Who fed them faithfully, and all the land
Directed with a just and equal hand.

PSALM LXXIX.

PART I. *Tune* 19.

THE Gentiles waste Thy Canaan, Lord,
  With fire and sword;
Thy holy temple they profane,
  With slaughter stain.
Beneath her ruins Salem groans,
Now nothing but a heap of stones.

The dead no funeral pomp attends,
  Nor weeping friends;
Their carcases our barbarous foes
  To beasts expose;
The rav'nous wolves become their tomb,
Or else the greedy vulture's womb.

With blood of saints the streams grow red,
  Like water shed;
Thy people now a general
  Reproach to all.
The Syrian and base Edomite
Deride, and in our woes delight.

How long, Lord, shall Thy jealous ire
  Devour like fire?
Thy anger, in a dreadful show'r
  Of vengeance, pour
On those who know not Thy great Name,
And think Thy worship but a shame.

PART II.

For they have laid our country waste,
          Our cities ras'd.
Lord, O remember not the crimes
          Of former times,
But for Thy tender mercy save
Our souls, now humbled to the grave!

Lord, for the glory of Thy Name,
          Redeem from shame.
O purge us, and propitious be!
          From thraldom free.
Why should the heathen thus blaspheme,
And say, Your God is but a dream?

Against them let Thy vengeance rise
          Before our eyes;
And for our blood shed by their guilt
          Let theirs be spilt.
O hear the sighing pris'ners' cry,
And save whom they have doom'd to die!

Our spiteful neighbours, Lord, deride
          Thee in their pride.
With sev'n-fold vengeance recompense
          Their insolence.
So we, Thy flock, our God will praise,
And to the stars Thy glory raise.

PSALM LXXX.

PART I.   *Tune 3.*

THOU Shepherd of Thy Israel,
    That, flock-like, leadest Joseph's race,
Who 'twixt the cherubims dost dwell,
    O hear! show Thy enlight'ning face.

Exalt Thy saving pow'r before
  Manasseh, Ephraim, Benjamin.
O from captivity restore,
  And let Thy beams upon us shine!
Great God of battle, wilt Thou still
  Be angry, and our pray'rs despise?
Bread steep'd in tears our stomachs fill,
  We drink the rivers of our eyes.
Our scoffing neighbours fall at strife
  Among themselves to share our right.
Great God, restore the dead to life,
  And comfort by Thy quick'ning light.

PART II.

This vine, from Egypt brought (the foe
  Expell'd) was planted by Thy Hand.
Thou gav'st it room and strength to grow,
  Until her branches fill'd the land.
The mountains took a shade from these,
  Which like a grove of cedars stood,
Extending to the Tyrian seas,
  And to Euphrates' rolling flood.
O why hast Thou her fences ras'd,
  Whilst ev'ry straggler pulls her fruit?
The browsing herd her branches waste,
  And salvage boars plough up her root.
Great God, return; this trampled vine
  From heav'n behold with mild aspéct,
Once planted by that Hand of Thine,
  The branches of Thy own elect.
Which now cut down wild flames devour,
  Through Thy fierce wrath to ruin brought.
Protect Thy people by Thy pow'r,
  And perfect what Thyself hath wrought.

Reviv'd, we will Thy Name adore,
Nor ever from Thy pleasure swerve.
O from captivity restore,
And by Thy pow'rful grace preserve!

PSALM LXXXI.

PART I. *Tune 7.*

O God our strength your voices raise,
In sacred numbers sing His praise.
The warbling lute, sweet viol, bring,
And solemn harp; loud timbrels ring.
The new moon seen, shrill trumpets sound,
Your sacred feasts with triumph crown'd.
These rites our God establishéd,
When Israel He from Egypt led;
Their necks with yokes of bondage wrung,
Inuréd to an unknown tongue.
Your burdens I have cast away,
Said He, and cleans'd your hands from clay;
Then sav'd, when in your fears you cried,
And from the thund'ring cloud replied.
I tried you; heard your murmurings,
At Meribah's admiréd springs.
You sons of Israel give ear,
I will instruct you, would you hear.
Beware, no foreign gods adore,
Nor their adult'rate pow'rs implore.

PART II.

I thee alone brought from the land
Of bondage with a mighty hand.
I know and will supply thy need,
When naked clothe, when hungry feed.

Yet would not they My counsel brook,
But desp'rately their God forsook.
Whom I unto their lusts resign'd,
And errors of their wand'ring mind.
O that they had My voice obey'd,
Nor from the paths of virtue stray'd!
Then victory their brows had crown'd,
Their slaughter'd foes had spread the ground.
Then had I made their enemy
Submit, and at their mercy lie ;
Themselves bless'd with eternal peace,
Enrichéd with the earth's increase ;
With flour of wheat and honey fill'd,
From breaches of the rock distill'd.

PSALM LXXXII.

Tune 4.

GOD sits upon the throne of kings,
And judges unto judgment brings.
  Why then so long
   Maintain you wrong,
And favour lawless things ?

Defend the poor, the fatherless,
Their crying injuries redress,
   And vindicate
   The desolate,
Whom wicked men oppress.

For they of knowledge have no light,
Nor will to know, but walk in night.
   Earth's bases fail ;
   No laws prevail;
Scarce one in heart upright.

Though gods and sons of the Most High,
Yet you like common men shall die,
　　Like princes fall.
　　Great God, judge all
The earth, Thy monarchy.

PSALM LXXXIII.

PART I.　　　　　　　　　　　*Tune* 1.

LORD, sit not still, as deaf unto our cries,
For lo! our enemies in tumults rise.
Ev'n those who Thy omnipotence deny,
And hate Thy Name, advance their crests on high;
Dark counsels take, and secretly contrive
Their slaughter, whom Thy mercy keeps alive.
Come, say they, let us with incessant strokes
Hew down this nation like a grove of oaks,
Till they no longer be, and Israel die
Both in his race and ruin'd memory.
They all in one confed'racy have made
A solemn league, supplied with foreign aid;
Fierce Idumæans, who in nomads stray,
And shaggy Ishmaelites that live by prey;
Th' incestuous race that border on the lake
Of salt Asphaltis; savage thieves, who take
Their name from servile Hagar; they who dwell
In Gebal; Ammonites who peace expell;
Stern Palestines, and wild Amalekites;
False Tyrians; Ashur with Lot's sons unites.

PART II.

Let them like Midian fall by mutual wounds;
Like Sisera; fall like Jabin on the bounds
Of Endor, where swift Kison takes his birth;
Who lay like dung upon the fatten'd earth.

Like Zeb and Oreb's princes, made a prey
For wolves; like Zeba and proud Zalmuna;
Who said, Let us these Israelites destroy,
And all the cities of their God enjoy.
O let them like a wheel be hurried round,
Like chaff which whirlwinds ravish from the ground;
As woods grown dry with age embrac'd with fire,
Whose flames above the singéd hills aspire.
So in the tempest of Thy wrath pursue,
And with Thy storms Thy trembling foes subdue.
O fill their hearts with grief, their looks with shame,
Till they invoke Thy late blasphemed Name.
Confound them with eternal infamy,
That they through anguish of their souls may die.
That men Jehovah's wonders may rehearse,
The Great Commander of this universe.

PSALM LXXXIV.
Tune 15.

 HOW amiable are
Thy abodes, Great God of war!
How I languish through restraint,
How my longing spirits faint!
Lord, for Thee I daily cry,
In Thy absence hourly die.
Sparrows there their young ones rear,
And the summer's harbinger[1]
By Thy altar builds her nest,
Where they take their envied rest.
O my King! O thou Most High!
Arbiter of victory!
Happy men, who spend their days
In Thy courts, there sing Thy praise.

---
[1] The Swallow.

Happy, who on Thee depend!
Thine their way, and Thou their end.
Who through Baca travelling,
Make that thirsty vale a spring;
Or soft show'rs from clouds distill,
And their empty cisterns fill.
Fresh in strength their course pursue,
Till they Thee in Sion view.
Lord of Hosts, incline Thine ear,
O Thou God of Jacob, hear!
Thou our Rock, extend Thy grace,
Look on Thy Anointed's Face.
One day in Thy courts alone
Far exceeds a million.
Let me be contemn'd and poor,
In Thy temple keep a door,
Than with wicked men possess
All that they call happiness.
O Thou Shield of our defence,
O Thou Sun, Whose influence
Sweetly glides into our hearts,
Thou, Who all to Thine imparts,
Happy, O thrice happy he,
Who alone depends on Thee!

PSALM LXXXV.

Tune 2.

AT length Thou hast Thy mercy shown,
Drawn from the Babylonian yoke;
Our sins remov'd which did provoke
Thy wrath; ev'n that now overblown.
Great God, our ruin'd state restore,
And let Thy anger flame no more.

O shall it like a comet reign,
  Extending to the yet unborn?
  Wilt Thou not quicken the forlorn,
That Thine in Thee may joy again?
  O show'r Thy mercy from above,
  Preserve and fix us in Thy love.

I will the voice of God attend,
  Who to His people speaks of peace.
  Such as in sanctity increase,
Nor to their sins again descend,
  These soon with freedom shall be bless'd,
  That glory may our land invest.

Those days shall consummate our bliss,
  Sweet clemency with truth shall meet,
  High justice gentle peace shall greet,
Saluting with a holy kiss;
  For truth shall from the earth arise,
  And righteousness look from the skies.

Then shall Jehovah distribute
  His blessings with a liberal hand;
  The rich and ever grateful land
Abundantly produce her fruit.
  For justice shall before Him go,
  And her fair steps to mortals show.

PSALM LXXXVI.

PART I. *Tune* 11.

MY God, Thy suppliant hear,
  Afford a gentle ear;
  For I am comfortless,
And labour in distress.

My righteous soul relieve,
So ready to forgive.
Thy servant, Lord, defend,
Whose hopes on Thee depend.
Me from the grave restore,
Who daily Thee implore.
From wasting sorrow free
The heart long vow'd to Thee.
For Thou art God alone,
To tender pity prone,
Propitious unto all
Who on Thy mercy call.
O hear my fervent pray'r,
And take me to Thy care;
Then ready to be found,
When troubles most abound.
What God like Thee, O Lord,
Of all by men ador'd;
Or underneath the sun
Such miracles hath done?

PART II.

Zeal shall all hearts inflame
T' adore and praise Thy Name,
For Thou art God alone,
Thy pow'r in wonders shown.
Direct me in Thy way,
So shall I never stray.
My thoughts from tempests clear,
United in Thy fear.
My soul shall celebrate
Thy praise, Thy pow'r relate,
That hast advanc'd my head,
And rais'd me from the dead.

The proud against me rise,
And pow'rful enemies
(All rebels to Thy will)
My guiltless blood would spill.
But O, Thou King of kings,
From Thee sweet mercy springs;
Still gracious, slow to wrath,
True to Thy servant's faith.
Lord, for Thy mercies' sake,
Into Thy bosom take;
Thy handmaid's son, O save
From the devouring grave!
Some happy sign expose
To my ashaméd foes,
That they Thy hate may see
To them, Thy love to me.

PSALM LXXXVII.
Tune 7.

THE Lord hath with His temple crown'd
Moriah, by His choice renown'd.
Not all the tents of Israel,
Or mountains which in height excell,
He so affects or celebrates
As lofty Sion's stately gates.
Jerusalem, thou throne of kings,
Of thee they utter glorious things.
Not by Judea's narrow bounds
Prescrib'd, the land which Nile surrounds,
Great Babylon, proud Palestine,
Rich Tyre which circling seas confine,
And black-brow'd Ethiopians,
Shall yield thee citizens and sons.

All sorts of people, foreign-bred,
As natives there indenizéd,
In Sion, built by immortal hands,
Firm as the mountain where it stands.
The Lord in His eternal scroll
Shall these as citizens enroll.
Their music shall th' affections raise,
And songs sung in Jehovah's praise;
Whose blessings on this city shall,
Like streams from heav'nly fountains, fall.

PSALM LXXXVIII.

PART I. *Tune* 19.

MY Saviour! both by night and day,
  To Thee I pray.
O let my cries transcend the spheres,
  And pierce Thy ears!
Lest sorrow stop my fainting breath,
Now near the jaws of greedy death.

My light extinguish'd, numberéd
  Among the dead;
Like men in battle slain, the womb
  Of earth their tomb;
Forgotten as if never known,
By Thy tempestuous wrath o'erthrown.

By Thee lodg'd in the lower deeps,
  Where horror keeps;
In dungeons where no sun displays
  His cheerful rays;
Crush'd by Thy wrath, on me Thy waves
Rush like so many rolling graves.

My old familiars, now my foes,
        Deride my woes;
My house becomes my gaol, where I
        In fetters lie;
Blind with my tears, with crying hoarse,
Hands rais'd in vain, a walking corse.

Wilt Thou to those Thy wonders show,
        Who sleep below?
The dead from their cold mansions raise,
        To sing Thy praise?
Shall mercy find us in the grave,
Or wilt Thou in destruction save?

Wilt Thou Thy wonders bring to light,
        In death's long night?
Or shall Thy justice there be shown,
        Where none are known?
I have, and still to Thee will pray,
Before the sun restore the day.

O why hast Thou withdrawn Thy grace,
        And hid Thy Face
From me, who from my infancy
        But daily die?
Whilst I Thy terrors undergo,
Distracted by these storms of woe.

Thy anger like a gulf devours
        My trembling pow'rs;
With troops of terrors circled round,
        In sorrow drown'd;
Depriv'd of those that lov'd me most,
To all in dark oblivion lost.

PSALM LXXXIX.

PART I. *Tune 22.*

UR grateful songs, O Thou Eternal King,
Shall ever of Thy boundless mercies sing,
And Thy unalterable truth rehearse
To after ages in a living verse.
For what is by Thy clemency decreed
Shall orderly and faithfully succeed;
Ev'n like those never resting orbs above,
Which on firm hinges circularly move.
Thus God unto His servant David swore,
This cov'nant made : I will for evermore
Thy seed establish and thy throne sustain,
Whilst seas shall flow, or moons increase and wane.
The heav'nly hierarchy Thy truth shall praise,
The saints below Thy glorious wonders blaze;
For who is like our God above the clouds,
Or who so great whom human frailty shrouds?
He to His angels terrible appears,
And daunts the tyrants of the earth with fears.
Great God! How great when dreadful armies join!
What God so strong, what faith so firm as Thine?

PART II.

Thy bounds the billows of the sea restrain,
Thou calm'st the tumults of th' incensèd main.
Proud Rahab, like a corse with blood imbru'd,
Hewn down, the strong with greater strength subdu'd.
Thine are the heav'ns, those lamps which gild the skies;
Round earth; broad seas, and all which they comprise.

Thou mad'st the southern and the northern pole
Whereon the orbs celestial swiftly roll.
Hermon invested with the morning rays,
And Tabor with the ev'ning's, sing Thy praise.
Thy Arm excells in strength, Thy Hands sustain
The world they made, and guide it with a rein.
Justice with judgment join'd Thy throne uphold,
Mercy and truth Thy sacred brows infold.
Thrice happy they who, when the trumpet calls,
Throng to Thy celebrated festivals!
They of Thy beauty shall enjoy the sight,
And guide their feet by that informing light.
Thy Name shall daily in their mouths be found,
And in Thy justice shall their joys abound.

PART III.

Our ornament in peace, our strength in wars,
Thy favour shall exalt us to the stars.
Thou Holy One of Israel, our King,
Thou our defence, secure beneath Thy wing!
Thus spake Jehovah by His prophet's voice:
Of strenuous David have I made My choice,
On that heroë pour'd My sacred oil,
To guide My people and preserve from spoil.
I will support him with My pow'rful arm,
No foe shall tribute force, nor treason harm.
His enemies before his face shall fly,
And those who hate his soul by slaughter die.
Our truth and clemency shall crown his days,
And to the firmament his glory raise.
He, from the billows of the Tyrian main,
To swift Euphrates shall extend his reign.
Who in his oft-renew'd devotions shall
Me Father, God, and Great Protector call.

My favourite he shall be, and My first birth,
Rais'd above all the princes of the earth.
My mercy him for ever shall preserve,
And from My promise I will never swerve.
His seed shall always reign; his throne shall last
While days have light, and nights their shadows cast.

PART IV.

If they My judgments slight, forsake My law,
My rites neglect, and from My rule withdraw,
Then I with whips will their offences scourge,
With labour, misery, and sorrows urge.
Yet will not utterly My king forsake,
My vow infringe, or alter what I spake.
I by My sanctity to David sware
That he and his should never want an heir,
To sway the Hebrew sceptre, while the sun
His usual race should through the zodiac run;
While men the moon and radiant stars should see,
The faithful witnesses of My decree.
But Thou art angry with Thy own elect,
And dost Thy late affected king reject;
Infringe the cov'nant to Thy servant sworn;
Thou from his brows his diadem hast torn,
Cast down the rampire which his strength renown'd,
And all his bulwarks levell'd with the ground;
Whom now his neighbours scorn, a common prey
And spoil to all that travel by the way.

PART V.

Thou addest strength and courage to his foes,
Who now rejoice and triumph in his woes;
Rebatest his sharp sword, unnerv'st his might,
And mak'st him shrink in fervour of the fight;

His splendour hast eclipséd, his renown
In ruins buried, and his throne cast down.
His youth consuméd with untimely age,
Mark'd out for shame, the object of Thy rage.
How long shall he in Thy displeasure mourn?
Still shall Thy anger like a furnace burn?
O call to mind the shortness of my days;
That dream of man, which like a flow'r decays.
Who lives that can the stroke of death defend,
Or shall not to the silent grave descend?
Where is Thy ancient love? Thy plighted troth,
Confirm'd to David by a solemn oath?
Remember the reproaches I have borne,
Those of the mighty, and their bitter scorn;
Traducéd, by Thy enemies abhorr'd.
Yet, O my pensive soul, praise thou the Lord!
      Amen, Amen.

A PARAPHRASE
UPON THE FOURTH BOOK OF THE PSALMS OF DAVID.

PSALM XC.

PART I. *Tune* 18.

THOU the Father of us all,
Our refuge from th' original,
   That wert our God, before
The aëry mountains had their birth,
Or fabric of the peopled earth,
   And art for evermore.

But frail man, daily dying, must
At Thy command return to dust;
   Or should he ages last,
Ten thousand years are in Thy sight
But like a quadrant of the night,
   Or as a day that's past.

He by Thy torrent swept from hence;
An empty dream, which mocks the sense,
   And from the fancy flies.
Such as the beauty of the rose,
Which in the dewy morning blows,
   Then hangs the head and dies.

Through daily anguish we expire;
Thy anger a consuming fire,
    To our offences due.
Our sins (although by night conceal'd,
By shame and fear) are all reveal'd,
    And naked to Thy view.

Thus in Thy wrath our years we spend,
And like a sad discourse they end,
    Nor but to seventy last;
Or if to eighty they arrive,
We then with age and sickness strive,
    Cut off with wingéd haste.

Part II.

Who knows the terror of Thy wrath,
Or to Thy dreadful anger hath
    Proportion'd his due fear?
Teach us to number our frail days,
That we our hearts to Thee may raise,
    And wisely sin forbear.

Lord, O how long! at length relent!
And of our miseries repent,
    Thy early mercy show;
That we may unknown comfort taste;
For those long days in sorrow past,
    As long of joy bestow.

The works of Thy accustom'd grace
Show to Thy servants; on their race
    Thy cheerful beams reflect.
O let on us Thy beauty shine!
Bless our attempts with aid Divine,
    And by Thy Hand direct.

PSALM XCI.

Tune 8.

WHO makes th' Almighty his retreat,
    Shall rest beneath His shady Wings,
Free from th' oppression of the great,
    The rage of war, or wrath of kings.
Free from the cunning fowler's train,
    The tainted air's infectious breath;
His truth in perils shall sustain,
    And shield thee from the stroke of death.
No terrors shall thy sleeps affright,
    Nor deadly flying arrows slay,
Nor pestilence devour by night,
    Or slaughter massacre by day.
A thousand and ten thousand shall
    Sink on thy right hand and thy left;
Yet thou secure shalt see their fall,
    By vengeance of their lives bereft.
Since God thou hast thy refuge made,
    And dost to Him thy vows direct,
No evil shall thy strength invade,
    Nor wasting plagues thy roof infect.
Thee shall His angels safely guide,
    Upheld by wingéd legións,
Lest thou at any time should'st slide,
    And dash thy foot against the stones.
Thou on the basilisk shalt tread,
    The mountain lion boldly meet,
And trample on the dragon's head,
    The leopard prostrate at thy feet.
Since he hath fix'd his love on Me,
    Saith God, and walkéd in My ways,
I will his soul from danger free,
    And from the reach of envy raise.

To him I his desires will give,
From danger guard, in honour place ;
He long, long happily shall live,
And flourish in My saving grace.

PSALM XCII.

PART I.   Tune 15.

THOU, Who art enthron'd above,
Thou, by Whom we live and move,
O how sweet, how excellent,
Is't with tongue and heart's consent,
Thankful hearts and joyful tongues,
To renown Thy Name in songs !
When the morning paints the skies,
When the sparkling stars arise,
Thy high favours to rehearse,
Thy firm faith, in grateful verse.
Take the lute and violin,
Let the solemn harp begin,
Instruments strung with ten strings,
While the silver cymbal rings.
From Thy works my joy proceeds,
How I triumph in Thy deeds !
Who Thy wonders can express ?
All Thy thoughts are fathomless ;
Hid from men in knowledge blind,
Hid from fools to vice inclin'd.
Who that tyrant sin obey,
Though they spring like flow'rs in May,
Parch'd with heat and nipt with frost,
Soon shall fade, for ever lost.

PART II.

Lord, Thou art most Great, most High;
Such from all eternity.
Perish shall Thy enemies,
Rebels that against Thee rise.
All, who in their sins delight,
Shall be scatter'd by Thy might.
But Thou shalt exalt my horn,
Like a youthful unicorn;
Fresh and fragrant odours shed
On Thy crownéd prophet's head.
I shall see my foes' defeat,
Shortly hear of their retreat.
But the just like palms shall flourish,
Which the plains of Judah nourish;
Like tall cedars mounted on
Cloud-ascending Lebanon.
Plants, set in Thy courts, below
Spread their roots, and upwards grow;
Fruit in their old age shall bring,
Ever fat and flourishing.
This God's justice celebrates;
He, my Rock, injustice hates.

PSALM XCIII.

Tune 21.

NOW Great Jehovah reigns,
    With majesty array'd;
His pow'r all pow'rs restrains,
    By men and gods obey'd.
      The round earth hung
        In liquid air;
      Establish'd there
      But by His tongue.

Thy throne more old than time,
And after, as before.
The floods in billows climb,
And foaming loudly roar.
With horrid noise
The ocean raves,
And breaks his waves
Against the skies.

But Thou, more to be fear'd,
More terrible than these;
Thy Voice in thunder heard,
Thy nod rebukes the seas.
Thee truth renowns;
Pure sanctity
Eternally
Thy temple crowns.

PSALM XCIV.

PART I. *Tune* 9.

GREAT God of Hosts, revenge our wrong
On those who are in mischief strong.
Upon Thy foes
Inflict our woes,
For vengeance doth to Thee belong.
Judge of the world, prevent
The proud and insolent.

How long shall they the just oppress,
And triumph in their wickedness?
How long supplant?
Ah! how long vaunt,

And glory in their dire success?
    Thy saints asunder break,
    Insulting o'er the weak!

Who strangers and poor widows kill,
The blood of wretched orphans spill,
        And say, Can He
        Or hear or see?
Doth God regard what's good or ill?
    Brute beasts, without a mind!
    O fools, in knowledge blind!

Shall not th' Almighty see and hear,
Who form'd the eye, and fram'd the ear?
        Who nations slew
        Not punish you?
Who taught, not know? to Him appear
    Dark counsels, secret fires,
    Vain hopes, and vast desires.

PART II.

But O! thrice blessed he, whom God
Chastiseth with his gentle rod;
        Informs, and awes
        By sacred laws;
In storms brought to a safe abode;
    While the unrighteous shall
    By wingéd vengeance fall.

For He will not forsake th' elect,
Nor who adore His Name reject;
        But judgment then
        Shall turn again
To justice, and her throne erect.
    Who are in heart upright
    Shall follow that clear light.

What mortal will th' afflicted aid,
Defend when impious foes invade?
    Lord, hadst not Thou,
    My soul ere now
In silent shades of death had laid;
    For He my out-cries heard,
    And from the centre rear'd.

When grief my lab'ring soul confounds,
Thou pourest balm into her wounds.
    Shall tyranny
    With Thee comply,
Who mischief for a law propounds?
    Who swarm to circumvent,
    And doom the innocent.

But Thou, O Lord, art my defence,
My refuge, and my recompence.
    The vicious shall
    By vices fall,
By their own sins be swept from hence.
    God shall cut off their breath,
    And give them up to death.

PSALM XCV.

Tune 18.

COME sing the Great Jehovah's praise,
    Whose mercies have prolong'd our days;
        Sing with a joyful voice.
With bending knees, and raiséd eyes
Adore your God; O sacrifice;
    In sacred hymns rejoice.

Great is the God of our defence,
Transcending all in eminence,
    His Hand the earth sustains ;
The depths, the lofty mountains made,
The land and liquid plains display'd,
    And curbs them with His reins.

O come, before His footstool fall,
Our only God, Who form'd us all,
    Through storms of danger led.
He is our Shepherd, we His sheep;
His Hands from wolves and rapine keep,
    In pleasant pastures fed.

The Voice of God thus spake this day :
Repine not as at Meribah,
    As in the wilderness ;
Where your forefathers tempted Me,
Who did My works of wonder see,
    And to their shame confess.

When vex'd for forty years, I said,
This people in their hearts have stray'd,
    Rebellious to command ;
To whom I in My anger swore,
That death should seize on them before
    They knew this pleasant land.

PSALM XCVI.

PART I.   *Tune* 15.

NEW composéd ditties sing
To our Everlasting King ;
    You, all you of human birth,
Fed and nourish'd by the earth,
Celebrate Jehovah's praise,
    Daily His deliv'ries blaze.

His glory let the Gentiles know,
To the world His wonders show.
O how Gracious! O how Great!
Earth His footstool, Heav'n His seat.
To be fear'd and honour'd more
Than those gods whom fools adore;
Idols by their servants made;
But our God the heav'ns display'd.
Honour, beauty, pow'r Divine,
In His sanctuary shine.
All, who by His favour live,
Glory to Jehovah give,
Glory due unto His Name,
And His mighty deeds proclaim.
Off'rings on His altar lay,
There your vows devoutly pay.

PART II.

In His beauteous holiness
To the Lord your pray'r address.
All whom earth's round shoulders bear,
Serve the Lord with joy and fear.
Tell mankind Jehovah reigns;
He shall bind the world in chains,
So as it shall never slide,
And with sacred justice guide.
Let the smiling heav'ns rejoice,
Joyful earth exalt her voice;
Let the dancing billows roar,
Echoes answer from the shore;
Fields their flow'ry mantles shake,
All shall in their joy partake;
While the woods' musicians sing
To the ever-youthful spring.

Fill His courts with sacred mirth;
He, He comes to judge the earth.
Justly He the world shall sway,
And His truth to men display.

PSALM XCVII.

Tune 7.

 EARTH! joy in Jehovah's reign;
You num'rous isles, clasp'd by the main.
Him rolling clouds and shades infold;
Judgment and truth His throne uphold.
Who fiery darts before Him throws,
With wingéd flames consumes His foes.
His light'ning made a day of night,
Earth trembl'd at so fear'd a sight.
The mountains at His Presence sweat,
Like pliant wax dissolv'd with heat,
At His descension from the sky,
Who rules the world's great monarchy.
The heav'ns declare His righteousness,
His glory wond'ring men confess.
Let those with shame to hell descend,
Whose knees to cursed idols bend,
Who rocks for deities implore.
O all you gods our God adore.
Rejoicing Sion heard her King,
Her daughters of His judgments sing,
Thou art exalted above all
Mankind, and Pow'rs angelical.
Those saints Thy shady wings protect,
Who sin abhor, and Thee affect.
For Thou hast sown the seeds of light,
And joy, which shall invest th' upright.
You just, your joyful hearts elate,
His blest memorial celebrate.

PSALM XCVIII.
Tune 21.

SING to the King of kings,
  Sing in unusual lays,
  That hath wrought wondrous things,
  His conquest crown with praise:
    Whose Arms alone,
      And Sacred Hands
      Their impious bands
    Have overthrown.

He justice brings to light;
  His saving truth extends,
Ev'n in the Gentiles' sight,
  To earth's remotest ends.
    His heav'nly grace
      At full display'd,
      And promise made
    To Jacob's race.

Let all that dwell on earth
  Their high affections raise,
With universal mirth,
  And loudly sing His praise;
    To music join
      The warbling voice,
      Let all rejoice
    With joy divine.

The sprightly trumpet sound,
  The shrill-voic'd cornet bring;
Let all with joy abound
  Before the Lord our King.
    Roar out you seas;
      You spangl'd skies,
      All you comprise,
    Rejoice with these.

Floods, clap your thronging waves;
You hills, exalt your mirth;
He, Who His people saves,
Now comes to judge the earth;
The round world shall
With justice try;
His equity
Dispens'd to all.

PSALM XCIX.

Tune 15.

LET our foes with terror quake,
Let the earth's foundations shake;
Now the Lord His reign begins,
Thron'd between the cherubins.
O how great in Sion's tow'rs!
High above all mortal pow'rs.
Great and terrible His Name;
Since so holy, praise the same.
Judgment His great pow'r affects,
Yet by equity directs.
These celestial twins embrace,
These reflect on Jacob's race.
O how Holy! above all
Honour, at His footstool fall.
Moses, Aaron, heretofore
Among those who mitres wore;
Samuel by vow desir'd,
Among those who were inspir'd;
These to Him their pray'rs preferr'd,
These by Him as soon were heard.
These His statutes rarely brake;
Unto these th' Almighty spake

In the pillar of a cloud,
To His service ever vow'd.
He did their petitions hear,
Merciful, and yet severe.
The Holy, on His holy hill
Glorify, and worship still.

PSALM C.

Tune 21.

ALL from the sun's uprise,
   Unto his setting rays,
   Resound in jubilees
The Great Jehovah's praise.
  Him serve alone;
   In triumph bring
   Your gifts, and sing
  Before His throne.

Man drew from man his birth,
  But God his noble frame
Built of the ruddy earth,
  Fill'd with celestial flame.
  His sons we are;
   Sheep by Him led,
   Preserv'd, and fed
  With tender care.

O to His portals press
  In your divine resorts;
With thanks His pow'r profess,
  And praise Him in His court
  How good! how pure!
   His mercies last;
   His promise past
  For ever sure!

PSALM CI.

Tune 20.

F justice I and mercy sing,
Which, Lord, from Thee their Fountain
    spring,
The graces that adorn a king.

Grave wisdom shall my steps direct,
No vice my heart nor roof infect.
When wilt Thou visit Thine elect?

No pleasure shall mine eyes misguide:
Who from the track of virtue slide,
Just hate shall from my soul divide.

Who mischief in their hearts contrive,
Delight in wrong, in factions strive,
I from my peaceful court will drive.

Who hath his friend with slander strook,
I will cut off; nor ever brook
A proud heart and a haughty look.

Mine eyes the faithful shall observe;
Those in My family shall serve,
Who never from pure virtue swerve.

But who are exercis'd in guile,
Whose tongues malicious lies defile,
I from my presence will exile.

And all the wicked in the land
Will cut off with a timely hand;
Nor shall they in God's city stand.

PSALM CII.

Part I.   *Tune* 14.

ACCEPT my pray'rs, nor to the cry
　Of mine afflictions stop Thine ear.
　Lord, in the time of misery
And sad restraint serene appear;
The sighings of my spirit hear;
　And when I call, with speed reply.

As smoke so fleets my soul away,
　My marrow dried as hearths with heat,
My heart struck down like wither'd hay,
　Through sorrow I forsake my meat,
　While meagre cares my liver eat;
The clinging skin my bones display.

Like desert-haunting pelicans,
　In cities not less desolate;
Like screech-owls, who with ominous strains
　Disturb the night, and daylight hate;
　A sparrow which hath lost his mate,
And on a pinnacle complains.

Reviling foes my honour blast,
　And frantic men my ruin swear.
For bread, I roll'd-on ashes taste,
　Each drop I drink mix'd with a tear.
　For, Lord, O who Thy wrath can bear?
Thou raisest, and dost headlong cast.

My days short as the ev'ning shade,
　As morning dew consume away;
As grass cut down with scythes I fade,
　Or like a flow'r cropp'd yesterday.
　But, Lord, Thou suffer'st no decay;
Thy promises shall never vade.

R

For Thou shalt from Thy rest arise,
  (Since now th' appointed time draws near)
And look on Sion's miseries,
  Her walls and batter'd buildings rear;
  Whose ruins to Thy saints are dear,
For they her dust as sacred prize.

PART II.

Thy Name, then, shall the Gentiles praise,
  All kings Thy honour celebrate;
For when the Lord shall Sion raise,
  His glory shall ascend in state:
  So prone to hear the desolate,
And succour them in all essays.

Unto eternal memory
  Our histories shall this record;
And all that are created by
  His pow'rful Hand shall fear the Lord;
  Who doth such grace to His afford,
And on the earth looks from on high;

To hear the pensive captives groan,
  The sons of Death by Him unbound;
His Name again in Sion known,
  That Salem may His praise resound;
  When in His service all the round
Of earth shall there be join'd in one.

Yet, Lord, amidst these hopes Thou hast
  Consum'd my strength, abridg'd my years;
Before my noon of life be past,
  Let me not die thus drown'd in tears.
  Time wastes not Thee, which all out-wears;
Thy happy days for ever last.

Thou mad'st the earth, Thou didst display
The heav'ns in various motion roll'd;
These and their glories shall decay,
But Thou shalt Thy existence hold;
They like a garment shall grow old,
And in their changes pass away.

But Thou art still the same; before
The world, and after shalt remain.
You blessed souls who God adore,
With patient hope your harms sustain;
For you shall prosper in His reign,
And yours subsist for evermore.

PSALM CIII.

PART I. *Tune 7.*

MY soul, and all my faculties,
Jehovah praise; sing till the skies
Re-echo His ascending fame:
My soul, O celebrate His Name!
Nor ever let the memory
Of His surpassing favours die.
He gently pardons our misdeeds,
And cures the wound which inward bleeds;
Hath from the chains of death unbound,
With clemency and mercy crown'd.
With food our hunger He subdues,
And eagle-like our youth renews.
His justice He extends to all;
Oppressors by His vengeance fall.
His sacred paths to Moses shown;
His miracles to Israel known.
From Him the springs of mercy flow;
Swift to forgive, to anger slow.

For He will not for ever chide,
Nor constant to His wrath abide;
But mildly from His rage relents,
And shortens our due punishments.
For as the heav'ns in amplitude
Exceed the centre they include,
So ample is His clemency
To all who on His grace rely.

PART II.

As far as the bright orient
Is distant from the sun's descent,
So far He sets from His aspéct
Their guilt who Him with fear affect;
And as a father to his child,
So soft, so quickly reconcil'd.
He knows the fabric of us all,
That dust is our original.
Man flourisheth like grass, a flow'r
That blows and withers in an hour,
By scorching heat, by blasting wind
Deflow'r'd, and leaves no print behind.
But His firm mercy shall embrace
His saints for ever, and their race;
Those who His equal laws fulfill,
Remember and perform His will.
In heav'n the Great Jehovah reigns,
And governs all that earth contains.
You angels who in strength exceed,
Who Him obey with wingéd speed,
You order'd hosts of radiant stars,
O you His flaming ministers,
All whom His wisdom did create,
Through His large empire celebrate
His glorious Name with sweet accord.
Join thou, my soul, to praise the Lord.

PSALM CIV.

PART I. *Tune* 22.

Y ravish'd soul, Great God, Thy praises sings,
Whom glory circles with her radiant wings,
And majesty invests than day more bright,
Cloth'd with the beams of new-created light.
He, like an all-enfolding canopy,
Fram'd the vast concave of the spangled sky,
And in the air-embracéd waters set
The basis of His hanging cabinet.
Who on the clouds as on a chariot rides,
And with a rein the flying tempest guides.
Bright angels His attendant spirits made,
By flame-dispersing seraphims obey'd.
The ever-fixéd earth cloth'd with the flood,
In whose calm bosom unseen mountains stood ;
At His rebuke it shrunk with sudden dread,
And from His Voice's thunder swiftly fled.
Then hills their late-concealéd heads extend,
And sinking valleys to their feet descend.
The trembling waters through their bottoms wind,
Till they the sea, their nurse and mother, find.
He to the swelling waves prescribes a bound,
Lest earth again should by their rage be drown'd.
Springs through the pleasant meadows pour their drills,
Which snake-like glide between the bord'ring hills,
Till they to rivers grow, where beasts of prey
Their thirst assuage, and such as man obey.

Part II.

In neighbouring groves the air's musicians sing,
And with their music entertain the spring.
He from celestial casement show'rs distills,
And with renew'd increase His creatures fills.
He makes the food-full earth her fruit produce,
For cattle grass, and herbs for human use.
The spreading vine long purple clusters bears,
Whose juice the hearts of pensive mortals cheers.
Fat olives smooth our brows with suppling oil,
And strength'ning corn rewards the reaper's toil.
His fruit-affording trees with sap abound.
The Lord hath Lebanon with cedars crown'd;
They to the warbling birds a shelter yield,
And wand'ring storks in lofty fir-trees build.
Wild goats to craggy cliffs for refuge fly,
And conies in the rocks' dark entrails lie.
He guides the changing moon's alternate face,
The sun's diurnal and his annual race.
'Twas He that made the all-informing light,
And with dark shadows clothes the aged night.
Then beasts of prey break from their mountain
    caves;
The roaring lion pinch'd with hunger craves
Food from His Hand; but when heav'ns greatest
    fire
Obscures the stars, they to their dens retire.
Men with the morning rise, to labour prest,[1]
Toil all the day, at night return to rest.

---

[1] *Prest*, i.e. ready.

Part III.

Great God ! how manifold, how infinite
Are all Thy works ! with what a clear fore-sight
Didst Thou create and multiply their birth !
Thy riches fill the far-extended earth ;
The ample sea, in whose unfathom'd deep
Innumerable sorts of creatures creep.
Bright scaléd fishes in her entrails glide,
And high built ships upon her bosom ride;
About whose sides the crooked dolphin plays,
And monstrous whales huge spouts of water raise.
All on the land, or in the ocean bred,
On Thee depend, in their due season fed.
They gather what Thy bounteous Hands bestow,
And in the summer of Thy favour grow.
When Thou contract'st Thy clouded brows, they mourn,
And dying, to their former dust return.
Again created by Thy quick'ning breath,
To re-supply the massacres of death.
No tract of time His glory shall destroy,
He in th' obedience of His works shall joy.
But when their wild revolts His wrath provoke,
Earth trembles, and the aëry mountains smoke.
I all my life will my Creator praise,
And to His service dedicate my days.
May He accept the music of my voice,
While I with sacred harmony rejoice.
Hence, you profane, who in your sins delight,
God shall extirp, and cast you from His sight.
My soul, bless thou this all-commanding King :
You saints and angels Hallelujah sing.

PSALM CV.

PART I. *Tune 22.*

O God, O pay your vows; invoke His Name,
And to the world His noble acts proclaim!
O sing His praises in immortal verse,
, And His stupendous miracles rehearse.
You saints rejoice, and glory in His grace;
His pow'r adore; for ever seek His Face.
Old Abraham's seed, you sons of the elect,
You Israelites, O you, who God affect,
Report the wonders by His finger wrought,
When in your cause th' inferior creatures fought.
Jehovah rules the many-peopled earth;
His judgment known to all of human birth.
He never will forget His promise past;
His covenants inviolable last,
Which He to faithful Abram made before,
And after to the holy Isaac swore;
To Jacob sign'd, confirm'd to Israel,
That their large offspring should in Canaan dwell.
When they, but few in number, wanderéd
In unknown regions, and their cattle fed,
He did their lives from violence protect,
And for their sakes ev'n mighty princes checkt.
Touch not, said He, my anointed; fear to wrong
Those sacred prophets who to Me belong.

PART II.

When raging famine in these climates reign'd,
He broke the staff of bread which life sustain'd.

But Joseph sent before them, sold to save
His brethren, by whose envy made a slave.
There for th' accuser's guilt in prison thrown,
With galling fetters bound for crimes unknown;
Tried with affliction, at the time decreed,
At once by Pharaoh both advanc'd and freed.
He of his household gave him the command,
And made him ruler over all his land;
His princes to his government subjects.
The prudent youth grave senators directs.
Then aged Jacob into Egypt came,
And sojourn'd in the fruitful fields of Ham.
God in that land His people multiplied;
Their foes, which now their greater strength envied,
Hate what they fear; He alienates their hearts,
To seek their ruin by deceitful arts.

PART III.

Then Moses on a sacred embassy
And Aaron sent, th' elect of the Most High.
There wrought His dreadful wonders, from the isle
Of sea-girt Pharos to the falls of Nile.
He bade Cimmerian darkness dim the day;
Th' assembled vapours His commands obey.
He their sev'n-channell'd waters turn'd to blood,
The fishes strangled in their native flood.
Frogs from the slimy earth in millions spring,
And skip about the chambers of the king.
All parts with swarms of noisome flies abound,
And lice, like quick'n'd dust, crawl on the ground.
He storms of killing hail for show'rs bestows,
And from the breaking clouds His light'ning throws.

Blasts all the vines and fig-trees in the land;
The woods with tempests torn or naked stand.
Innumerable locusts these succeed,
And caterpillars on their leavings feed.
They bite the tender herb, the bud and flow'r,
And all the verdure of the earth devour.
Their strength (the first-born) slew; which fill'd their ears
With female screeches, and their hearts with fears.

PART IV.

Then He the Hebrews out of Goshen brought
In able health, with gold and silver fraught.
Th' inhabitants, whose tears augment the Nile,
At their departure joy, and fear exile.
A cloud to shade them from the sun was spread,
And nightly by a flaming pillar led.
At their request He sends them show'rs of quails,
And bread from heav'n, like coriander, hails.
Cleaves the hard rocks, from whence a fountain flows,
And unknown rivers to those deserts shows.
For He His sacred promise call'd to mind,
To Abraham His friend and servant sign'd.
Thus He His people brought from servitude,
Whose long-felt miseries in joy conclude.
From hence the heathen by our weapons chas'd,
And us His sons in their possessions plac'd,
That from His statutes we might never swerve.
O praise the Lord, and Him devoutly serve.

PSALM CVI.

PART I.   *Tune* 22.

WITH grateful hearts Jehovah's praise resound,
In goodness Great, Whose mercy hath no bound.
What language can express His mighty deeds,
Or utter His due praise which words exceeds?
Thrice blessèd they who His commands observe,
Nor ever from the track of justice swerve.
Great God! O with benevolent aspéct
(Ev'n with the love Thou bear'st to Thine elect)
Behold and succour; that my ravish'd eyes
May see a period of their miseries,
Who Thee adore; that I may give a voice
To Thy great acts, and in their joy rejoice.
We, as our fathers, have Thy grace exil'd,
Revolted, and our souls with sin defil'd.
They, of Thy miracles in Egypt wrought,
So full of fear and wonder, never thought;
Thy mercies, than their hairs in number more;
But murmur'd on the Erythræan shore.
Yet for His honour sav'd them from the foe,
That all the world His wondrous pow'r might know.
There the commanded sea asunder rent,
While Israel through his dusty channel went.
Whom He from Pharaoh and his army saves,
The swift-returning floods their fatal graves.

Part II.

Then they His word believ'd, and sung His
  praise;
Yet soon forgot, and wander'd from His ways.
Who long for flesh to pamper their excess,
And tempt Him in the barren wilderness.
He grants their wish, and, with a flight of fowls,
Sent meagre death into their hungry souls.
They Moses' gentle government oppose,
And envy Aaron whom the Lord had chose.
The yawning earth then in her silent womb
Did Dathan and Abiram's troops entomb.
A swiftly-spreading fire among them burns,
And those conspirators to ashes turns.
Yet they, the slaves of sin, in Horeb made
A calf of gold, and to an idol pray'd.
The Lord, their glory, thus exchangéd they
For th' image of a beast that feeds on hay;
Forgot their Saviour, all His wonders shown
In Zoan, and the plains by Nile o'erflown;
The wonders acted by His pow'rful Hand,
Where the Red Sea obey'd His stern command.
God had pronounc'd their ruin : Moses then,
His servant Moses, and the best of men,
Stood in the breach which their rebellion made,
And by his pray'r the Hand of vengeance stay'd.

Part III.

Yea they this fruitful Paradise despis'd,
Nor His so-oft confirméd promise priz'd,
But mutiniéd against their faithful guide,
And basely wish'd they had in Egypt died.
For this the Lord advanc'd His dreadful Hand,
To overthrow them on th' Arabian sand;

To scatter their rebellious seed among
Their foes, expos'd to poverty and wrong.
Besides, Baal-Peor they ador'd, and fed
On sacrifices offer'd to the dead.
Thus their impieties the Lord incense,
Who smote them with devouring pestilence.
But when with noble anger Phinees slew
The bold offenders, He His plagues withdrew.
This was reputed for a righteous deed,
Which should for ever consecrate his seed.
So they at Meribah His anger mov'd,
The sacred prophet for their sakes reprov'd.
Their cries his saint-like sufferance provoke,
Who rashly in his soul's distemper spoke,
Nor ever enter'd the affected land.
They, still rebellious to Divine Command,
Preserv'd those nations by His wrath subdu'd,
Mix'd with the heathen, and their sins pursu'd;
Their cursèd idols serve with rites profane,
(Snares to their soul) and from no crime abstain.

PART IV.

Their sons and virgin-daughters sacrifice
To devils, and look on with tearless eyes.
Defil'd the land with innocent blood, which sprung
From their own loins on flaming altars flung.
Unto adulterate deities they pray'd,
And worshippèd those gods their hands had made.
These crying sins exasperate the Lord,
Who now His own inheritance abhorr'd.
Giv'n up unto the heathen for a prey;
Slaves to their foes; who hate them most, obey.
Deliver'd oft; as oft His wrath provoke,
And with increasing sins renew their yoke.

Yet He compassionates their miseries,
And with soft pity hears their mournful cries.
His former promise calls to mind, relents,
And in His mercy of His wrath repents.
In savage hearts unknown compassion bred,
By whom but lately into thraldom led.
Great God of gods, Thy votaries protect,
And from among the barbarous re-collect!
That we to Thee may dedicate our days,
And jointly triumph in Thy glorious praise.
Blest, O for ever blest, be Israel's King:
All you His people, Hallelujah sing.
                              Amen, Amen.

A PARAPHRASE
UPON THE FIFTH BOOK OF THE PSALMS OF DAVID.

PSALM CVII.

PART I. *Tune 7.*

XTOLL, and our good God adore,
Whose sea of mercy hath no shore.
O you by tyrants late oppress'd,
Now from your servile yokes re-
leas'd,
Praise Him Who your redemption wrought,
And home from barbarous nations brought.
From where the morn her wings displays,
From where the ev'ning crowns the days;
Beneath the burning zone, and near
The influence of the freezing bear.
They in unpeopled deserts stray'd,
The heav'ns their roof, the clouds their shade.
Their souls with thirst and hunger faint;
None by, to pity their complaint.
When to the Lord their God they cried,
His mercy their extremes supplied.
He led them through the wilderness,
And gave them cities to possess.

A PARAPHRASE UPON

O you, His goodness celebrate,
His acts to all the world relate !
For He in foodless deserts fed
The hungry with celestial bread.
From wond'ring rocks new currents roll,
To satisfy the thirsty soul.

Part II.

Those rebels who His counsel slight,
Imprison'd in the shades of night;
Horrors of guilt their souls surprise;
When humbled with their miseries,
They to the Lord address'd their pray'rs,
His mercy comforts their despairs,
From darkness draws, dissolves their gyves,[1]
And from Death's jaws preserves their lives.
O you, His goodness celebrate,
His acts to all the world relate!
He breaks steel-bars and gates of brass,
To force a way for His to pass.
Those fools, whom pleasing sins entice,
Are punish'd by their darling vice.
Their souls all sorts of food distaste,
Whom troops of pale diseases waste.
When they to God direct their pray'rs
His mercy comforts their dispairs ;
His word restores them from their graves,
And from a dreadful ruin saves.
O you, His goodness celebrate,
His acts to all the world relate !

---

[1] The 8vo. of 1676 reads *grieves*, but the folio of 1638 has *Gieves*, which is doubtless *gyves*, and rhymes with *lives*.

Due praises to His altar bring,
And of your great redemption sing.

PART III.

Who sail upon the toiling main,
And traffic in pursuit of gain,
To such His pow'r is not unknown,
Nor wonders in the ocean shown.
At His command black tempests rise;
Then mount they to the troubled skies,
Thence sinking to the depths below,
The ship hulls as the billows flow;
And all aboard at ev'ry seel,
Like drunkards, on the hatches reel.
When they to God direct their pray'rs
His mercy comforts their despairs.
Forthwith the bitter storms assuage,
And foaming seas suppress their rage:
Then, singing, with a prosp'rous gale,
To their desiréd harbour sail.
O you His goodness celebrate,
His acts to all the world relate!
His fame in your assemblies raise,
And in the sacred senate praise.

PART IV.

He rivers turns t' a wilderness,
Springs dried up by the sun's access.
To scourge their sins, He makes the soil
Ungrateful to the owner's toil;
Turns sandy deserts into pools,
And parchéd earth with fountains cools.
There plants His hungry colonies,
Where strongly-fencéd cities rise.

The fields their yellow mantles wear,
And spreading vines full clusters bear.
They infinitely multiply,
Their herds of no diseases die.
But when their sins His wrath incense,
Then famine, war, and pestilence
Their miserable lives devour.
Their princes He deprives of pow'r,
Who in the pathless wilderness
Conceal'd themselves from man's access.
The poor He raiseth from the ground;
Their families like flocks abound.
The just shall this with joy behold;
Th' unjust with fear and shame controll'd.
The wise these changes will record,
That they may know and serve the Lord.

PSALM CVIII.

Tune 2.

MY thoughts the Lord their object make;
  Before the ruddy morning spring
  My glory of His praise shall sing;
Awake my lute, my harp awake,
  While I to all the world rehearse
  His praises in a living verse.

Thy mercy (O how great!) extends
  Above the starry firmament,
  Still unto tender pity bent:
Thy truth the soaring clouds transcends,
  Thy head above the heav'ns erect,
  Thy glory on the earth reflect.

O hear us, who Thy aid implore,
  And with Thy own right Hand defend;
  To Thy belovéd succour send.

God by His sanctity thus swore :—
　I Succoth's valley will divide,
　In Sichem's spoils be magnified.
Manasseh, Gilead, both are Mine ;
　Ephraim My strength, in battle bold ;
　Thou, Judah, shalt My sceptre hold.
I will triumph o'er Palestine ;
　Base servitude shall Moab waste ;
　O'er Edom I My shoe will cast.

Who will our forward troops direct
　To Rabbah strongly fortified,
　Or into sandy Edom guide ?
Lord, wilt not Thou, that didst reject,
　Nor wouldst before our armies go,
　Now lead our host against the foe ?
When death and horror most affright,
　Do Thou our troubled souls sustain,
　For O, the help of man is vain !
Lead, and we valiantly shall fight.
　Thy Feet our foes shall trample down,
　Thy Hands our brows with conquest crown.

PSALM CIX.

Part I. *Tune 1.*

MY God, my Glory, leave not in distress,
　　Nor let prevailing fraud the truth oppress.
They who delight in subtleties and wrongs,
Afflict me with the poison of their tongues ;
With slander and detraction gird me round,
And would, without a cause, my life confound.
Good turns with evil proudly recompense,
And love with hate ; my merit, my offence.

But I in these extremes to Thee repair,
And pour out my perplexéd soul in pray'r.
Subject him to a tyrant's stern command,
Subverting Satan place at his right hand;
Found guilty when arraign'd; in that fear'd time
Let his rejected pray'rs augment his crime.
May he by violence untimely die,
And let another his command supply.
Let his distresséd widow weep in vain,
His wretched orphans to deaf ears complain.
Let them the wand'ring paths of exile tread,
And in unpeopled deserts seek their bread.
Let griping usurers divide his spoil,
And strangers reap the harvest of his toil.

PART II.

In his long mis'ry may he find no friend,
None to his race so much as pity lend.
Let his posterity be overthrown,
Their names to the succeeding age unknown.
Let not the Lord his father's sins forget,
His mother's infamy before him set.
O let them be the object of His eye,
Till He out-root their hated memory;
That to the wretched would no mercy show,
But cruelly pursu'd his overthrow;
Laid trains to kill the broken and contrite.
On his own head let his dire curses light.
He hated blessing, never be he blest;
Let cursing, like a robe, his loins invest,
And like a fatal girdle gird him round,
As he with execrations did abound.
Let them, like water, in his bowels boil,
And eat into his bones like burning oil.
Thus let the Lord reward my enemies,
Who seek to blast me with malicious lies.

THE PSALMS OF DAVID.

Part III.

But, Lord, in my deliverance proclaim
Thy mercy, for the honour of Thy Name.
For I am poor, with misery oppress'd,
My wounded heart bleeds in my panting breast.
I like the ev'ning shadow am declin'd,
And like the locust toss'd with ev'ry wind.
My feeble knees beneath their burden bend,
My flesh with fasting falls, my bones ascend.
Reproach hath seiz'd on me; my foes revile,
And in derision shake their heads, and smile.
My God, O snatch me from the swallowing grave!
Thy servant with accustom'd mercy save;
That they may know it was Thy pow'rful Hand,
And how I by Divine supportance stand.
Still may they vainly curse whom Thou dost bless,
And pine with envy at my good success.
Let them be cloth'd with shame: O be their own
Confusion on them like a mantle thrown.
But I Thy praise will duly celebrate,
And to the multitude Thy deeds relate,
That hast th' afflicted soul from sorrow freed,
And from their snares who had his death decreed.

PSALM CX.
Tune 18.

THE Lord unto my Lord thus spake:—
Sit at My right Hand, till I make
A foot-stool of Thy foes.
He will Thy rod from Sion send,
Unto Whose pow'r all pow'rs shall bend,
That dare Thy rule oppose.

262   A PARAPHRASE UPON

Thy people willingly shall pay
Their vows in that triumphant day,
    With their united pow'rs,
Array'd in ephods; nor so few
As are those pearls of morning-dew,
    Which hang on herbs and flow'rs.

He swore, Who never oath did break,
Of the order of Melchisedek
    That Thou a priest should'st reign;
Ev'n while the sun dispers'd his light,
While moons shall rule th' alternate night,
    Or stars their course maintain.

God, in that day at Thy right hand,
Their blood, who tyrant-like command,
    Shall in His fury spill:
He in His justice shall confound
The heathen, and the purple ground
    With heaps of slaughter fill.

Who over many nations sway,
And only their own wills obey,
    Shall sink beneath His rage:
Then shall this all-subduing King,
With water of the crystal spring,
    His burning thirst assuage.

PSALM CXI.

Tune 23.

Y soul the honour of our King
Shall in the great assembly sing.
Great are the wonders He hath shown,
With joy by their admirers known.

His glorious deeds all praise transcend,
His equal justice knows no end;
Left in eternal monuments,
Whose mercy death and hell prevents;
Feeds those who fear His Name, and will
His promise faithfully fulfill.
Who planted with a pow'rful Hand
His people in this pleasant land.
Just judgment executes, directs
By sacred laws, and truth affects.
These fretting time shall never waste,
But squar'd by justice ever last.
His word to us confirm'd by deed,
So often from oppression freed.
His Name is terrible to all,
His fear is the original
Of wisdom; and they only wise
Who make His laws their exercise.
His praise, while men have memory,
And pow'r of speech, shall never die.

PSALM CXII.

HALLELUJAH. *Tune* 23.

THAT man is blest who fears the Lord,
And cheerfully obeys His word.
His seed shall flourish on the earth,
Their offspring happy from their birth.
His house with riches shall abound,
His truth with endless honour crown'd.
To him in darkness light ascends,
Mild, gracious, just in all his ends.
His bounty for the poor provides,
Discretion all his actions guides.

No violence shall cast him down,
No time deface his just renown,
Nor rumours shake his confidence,
The Lord his Hope, and strong Defence.
Confirm'd in fearless fortitude,
Till he have all his foes subdu'd.
He the necessitated feeds.
The honour of his virtuous deeds
Shall live in sacred memory,
His glories shall ascend on high.
Th' unjust, enrag'd, their teeth shall grind,
And languish with the grief of mind;
Pale envy shall their flesh consume,
And all their hopes convert to fume.

PSALM CXIII.

HALLELUJAH.   *Tune* 23.

 YOU, who serve the living Lord,
Due praises to His Name afford.
Now and for ever celebrate;
Let all His noble acts relate,
Ev'n from the purple morn's uprise
To where the ev'ning flecks the skies.
All pow'r to His dominion bends;
His glory the bright stars transcends.
What god can be compar'd with ours,
Who, thron'd in heav'n's superior tow'rs,
Submits Himself to guide and move
All that is done in heav'n above;
And from that height vouchsafes to throw
His eyes on us, who creep below?
The poor He raiseth from the dust,
Ev'n from the dunghill lifts the just,

Whom He to height of honour brings,
And sets him in the thrones of kings.
He fructifies the barren womb;
The childless, mothers now become.

HALLELUJAH.

PSALM CXIV.

Tune 23.

WHEN Israel left th' Egyptian land,
Freed from a tyrannous command,
God His own people sanctified,
And He Himself became their Guide.
Th' amazèd seas, this seeing, fled,
And Jordan shrunk into his head.
The cloudy mountains skipp'd like rams,
The little hills like frisking lambs.
Recoiling seas, what caus'd your dread?
Why, Jordan, shrunk'st thou to thy head?
Why, mountains, did you skip like rams?
And why, you little hills, like lambs?
Earth, tremble thou before His Face,
Before the God of Jacob's race;
Who turn'd hard rocks into a lake,
When springs from flinty entrails brake.

PSALM CXV.

PART I. *Tune 8.*

WE nothing can of merit claim;
Not for our sakes Thy aid afford,
But for the honour of Thy Name,
Thy mercy, and unfailing word.

Why should th' insulting heathen cry,
    Where's now the God they vainly praise?
Our Lord, enthron'd above the sky,
    All underneath at pleasure sways.
Their gods but gold and silver be,
    Made by a frail artificer;
For they have eyes that cannot see,
    Dumb mouths, and ears that cannot hear.
Fools on their altars incense throw,
    Who nothing smell; their feet are bound,
Nor have they pow'r to move or go;
    Their throats give passage to no sound.
Their hands can neither give nor take,
    Unapt to punish or defend;
As senseless they who idols make,
    Or to their carvéd statues bend.

PART II.

Your hopes on God, O Israel, place,
    He is your Help and strong Defence;
Be He, you priests of Aaron's race,
    The object of your confidence.
In Him, all you that fear Him, trust,
    He shall protect you in distress;
The Lord is of His promise just,
    And will His faithful servants bless.
The house of chosen Israel,
    And Aaron's holy family,
The poor, and who in pow'r excell,
    That love, and on His aid rely,
They shall a mighty people grow,
    Their children happy from their birth.
He will increase of gifts bestow,
    Whose Hand created heav'n and earth.
He in the heav'n of heav'ns resides,

And over all His creatures reigns,
Among the sons of men divides
The earth, and all the earth contains.
Who sleep within the vaults of death
No off'rings to His altars bring;
O praise His Name, while we have breath,
And loudly Hallelujah sing.

PSALM CXVI.

Tune 4.

Y soul entirely shall affect
The Lord, Whose ears my groans respect.
In misery
He heard thy cry;
To Him thy pray'rs direct.

Sorrows of death my soul assail'd,
The greedy jaws of hell prevail'd;
Depress'd with grief,
When all relief
And human pity fail'd,

I cried: My God, O look on me,
Thou ever just th' afflicted free:
O from the grave
Thy servant save;
For mercy lives in Thee.

The innocent, and long distrest,
The humble mind by wrongs opprest,
Thy favour still
Preserves from ill:
My soul, then, take thy rest.

God stay'd my feet and dried my tears,
Redeem'd from death and deadly fears;

That still I might
Walk in His sight,
And number many years.

Thus with a firm belief I pray'd :
Yet in extremes of trouble said :—
All on the earth
Of mortal birth,
Ev'n all of lies are made.

What shall I unto God restore
For all His mercies ? Fall before
His holy throne,
And Him alone
With sacred rites adore.

I will perform my vows this day,
Where they frequent who God obey.
Right precious is
The death of His :
He sees, and will repay.

Lord, I am Thine, Thy hand-maid's seed ;
By Thee from raging tyrants freed.
My praise shall rise
In sacrifice ;
My thanks Thy altar feed.

I will perform my vows this day,
Where they frequent who God obey :
Ev'n in his court,
Within thy fort,
Renownéd Solyma.

THE PSALMS OF DAVID.

PSALM CXVII.
Tune 21.

YOU nations of the earth,
    Our Great Preserver praise.
All you of human birth,
    To heav'n His glory raise.
        Whose mercy hath
        No end nor bound:
        His promise crown'd
    With constant faith.

PSALM CXVIII.

PART I.   *Tune* 23.

PRAISE our Good God, that King of kings,
From whom eternal mercy springs.
Let Israel, let Aaron's race,
Let all that flourish in His grace,
Confess, that from the King of kings
Eternity of mercy springs.
He in my trouble heard my pray'rs,
And freed me from their deadly snares.
He fights my battles, then how can
I fear the pow'r of feeble man?
Assists my friends; my enemies
Shall with their slaughter feast mine eyes.
Far better to have confidence
In God, than trust to man's defence:
On Him much safer to rely,
Than on the strength of monarchy.

The nations all at once assail'd,
But by His aid my sword prevail'd.
Their armies had beset me round,
I with their bodies strew'd the ground.
Though they like bees about me swarm,
His holy Name and pow'rful Arm
Shall soon consume their num'rous pow'rs,
As fire the crackling thorn devours.

PART II.

Mad men ! his fall you seek in vain,
Whom Great Jehovah's Hands sustain.
He is my strength; His praise my song;
By Him preserv'd from pow'rful wrong.
Our tents with public joy shall ring,
The just of their deliv'rance sing.
He with His own right Hand hath fought,
His own right Hand hath wonders wrought,
I shall not die, but live to praise
The Lord, Who hath prolong'd my days.
He with a scourge my sin corrects,
Yet from the darts of death protects.
You to His service sanctified,
The temple doors set open wide,
That I may enter in His Name,
And celebrate His glorious fame.
Those are the doors, at which all they
Shall enter, who His will obey.
His praise with hymns immortalize !
My Saviour, Who hath heard my cries.

PART III.

That stone the builders from them cast,
Is highest on the corner plac'd.
God hath reveal'd these mysteries,
So full of wonder, to our eyes.

This is His day, a day of joy,
Of everlasting memory.
Great God of gods, Thy king protect,
Propitious prove to Thy elect.
O blest be he whom God shall send!
We, who within his courts attend,
You from His sanctuary bless,
And daily pray for your success.
God, ev'n the Lord, hath shed His light
Into our souls, and clear'd our sight.
Bind to the altar's horns a lamb,
New-weanéd from the bleating dam.
Thou art my God; my songs shall praise,
And to the stars Thy glory raise.
Praise our Good God, the King of kings,
From Whom eternal mercy springs.

PSALM CXIX.

Part I. *Tune 1.*

ALEPH.

BLEST are the undefil'd who God obey,
 Seek with their hearts, nor from His
  precepts stray.
No tempting vice shall those from virtue draw,
Who with unfainting zeal observe His law.
Lord, by Thy sacred rule my steps direct.
Those shall not blush who Thy commands affect.
Thy justice learnt, my soul shall sing Thy praise.
Forsake me not, O guide me in Thy ways.

Part II.

BETH.

Young man, thy actions by His precepts guide;
From these let not Thy zealous servant slide.

A PARAPHRASE UPON

Thy word, writ in my heart, shall curb my will.
O teach me how I may Thy laws fulfill!
Those by Thy tongue pronounc'd I will unfold.
Thy testaments by me more priz'd than gold.
On these I meditate, admire; there set
My soul's delight; these never will forget.

PART III.
GIMEL.

O let me live t' observe Thy laws: mine eyes
Illuminate to view those mysteries.
Me, a poor pilgrim, with Thy truth inspire,
For Whom my soul ev'n fainteth with desire.
The proud is curs'd, who from Thy precepts strays.
Bless and preserve my soul, which these obeys.
No hate of princes from Thy law deters:
My study, my delight, my counsellers.

PART IV.
DALETH.

My down-cast soul, as Thou hast promis'd, raise.
Thou know'st my thoughts, direct me in Thy ways.
Inform, and I Thy wonders will profess.
O strengthen me that labour in distress!
Shew Thy clear paths, false error's mist remov'd.
I have Thy chosen truth and judgments lov'd.
To these I cleave; O shield me from disgrace.
Enlarge my heart to run that heav'nly race.

PART V.
HE.

Teach Thou, and I Thy statutes will observe;
Nor from that sacred knowledge ever swerve.

THE PSALMS OF DAVID.

My soul to those delightful paths confine;
From avarice purge, and to Thy laws incline.
Divert from vain desires, my darkness clear;
Confirm the soul devoted to Thy fear.
Free from fear'd shame. Thy judgments are upright.
O quicken me who in Thy word delight.

PART VI.

VAU.

His soul protect who on Thy word relies,
And silence my reproachful enemies.
O Thou my hope, in me Thy truth preserve,
So I Thy laws for ever shall observe;
Will freely walk in Thy affected way,
Will boldly before kings Thy truth display;
For in Thy statutes I my comfort place,
Those study, love, and with my soul embrace.

PART VII.

ZAIN.

Think of Thy promise which my hopes hath fed,
All storms appeas'd, and rais'd me from the dead.
Nor for proud scoffs have I Thy laws declin'd;
Confirm'd, when I Thy judgments call to mind.
They, who Thy laws desert, incense my rage:
Sung in the mansion of my pilgrimage.
Thy Name, Great God, I prais'd, when others slept;
This comfort had, since I Thy statutes kept.

PART VIII.

CHETH.

Thou art my portion: I will Thee adore,
Thy laws observe, and promis'd grace implore.

My actions by Thy sacred rules direct,
And Thy commands with forward zeal effect.
The wicked rob, but I Thy statutes prize;
At midnight to applaud Thy justice rise.
Who fear and keep Thy laws, such are my friends.
Instruct; Thy mercy through the world extends.

Part IX.

TETH.

Thou to Thy servant hast perform'd Thy word:
Discerning knowledge to his faith afford.
Thou Sea of Goodness, that my soul conforms
Unto Thy statutes by affliction's storms.
The proud, fat at the heart, base slanders raise;
But I will trust in Thy affected ways.
Me bless'd affliction to Thy courts hath brought.
Thy laws more priz'd than ships with treasure
    fraught.

Part X.

JOD.

Inform me, my Creator, in Thy laws,
That Thine may see Thy observer with applause.
Thou, Ever-just, in favour dost correct.
With promis'd mercy comfort Thine elect.
That I may live, who in Thy precepts joy;
Those keep: the proud, who causeless hate, destroy.
Who fear and know Thy laws, to me unite:
O, lest I perish, guide me by their light!

PART XI.
CAPH.

With expectation faint, and blind, yet still
My soul expects. Thy promise, Lord, fulfill.
I, though a bladder, on Thy word depend.
Confound my foes; when shall my sorrows end?
The proud have pitch'd their toils, infring'd Thy
   laws:
O Sacred Justice, snatch me from their jaws!
They had almost devour'd, but I affect
Thy precepts: quicken, and by those direct.

PART XII.
LAMED.

Thy faithful promises are fix'd above,
Firm as the poles, or earth, which never move;
By Thy eternal ordinance dispos'd.
Thy laws my life; else grief my eyes had clos'd.
Nor will I these forget; by these renew'd.
Thy chosen save, who hath Thy truth pursu'd.
The wicked chase my soul, which Thee obeys:
Thy word shall last when heav'n and earth de-
   cays.

PART XIII.
MEM.

O how I love Thy laws! those exercise!
By them made wiser than my enemies.
More than my teachers know, more than the old;
With virtue these inflame, from vice withhold.
That they may guide me, I have cleans'd my heart,
And from Thy precepts never will depart;

Than Hermon's honey to my taste more sweet.
By-ways I hate; by Thine become discreet.

PART XIV.
NUN.

Thy word my light; a lamp to guide my way.
I sware t'observe Thy truth, and will not stray.
My wounded soul with promis'd mercy heal;
Accept my off'rings, and Thy will reveal.
Although inclos'd with death, though foes have laid
Snares for my soul, yet have I Thee obey'd.
My comforts, my eternal heritage:
O may I keep them till I die through age!

PART XV.
SAMECH.

I love Thy law, my hate to sin is great:
O Thou, my hope, my shield, my safe retreat!
My will shall Thine obey. Hence, you profane!
Lord, save my soul, nor let me hope in vain.
Uphold, and I Thy justice shall applaud.
Thou hast entrapp'd Thy foes in their own fraud,
Cast out like dross. My heart affects Thy path,
Yet trembles with the horror of Thy wrath.

PART XVI.
AIN.

O leave me not to my outrageous foes,
Nor to their scorn my righteous soul expose.
Mine eyes ev'n fail while I Thy aid expect.
Be merciful, and in Thy ways direct.

Enlarge my mind Thy ways to understand:
'Tis time ; for they infringe Thy just command,
Which more than gold, than gold refin'd I prize;
In all upright.   But hate deceitful lies.

PART XVII.

PE.

Thy Word, the Gate of Life, ev'n babes inspires
With knowledge; this my obsequious soul admires :
This I with thirsty appetite devour.
Thy streams of mercy on Thy servant pour.
Compose my steps, so shall not sin subject,
Nor man oppress ; for I Thy laws affect.
Shine on my soul, Thy statutes teach: mine eyes
Shed show'rs of tears when men Thy laws despise.

PART XVIII.

TSADDI.

As Thou Thyself, so all Thy laws are just,
Faithful to those who in Thy promise trust.
Zeal hath consum'd me, for my foes' neglect
Of Thy pure laws, which I in heart affect.
Those to observe, though mean and scorn'd, intend.
Truth crowns Thy word ; Thy justice without end.
These in my grief and trouble comfort give.
Inform with knowledge, that my soul may live.

PART XIX.

COPH.

O hear my cries ! preserve his life, who will
Thy laws obey, and just commands fulfill.

My eyes out-watch the night; my cries prevent
The early morn, in due devotion spent.
Hear, and revive; Thy justice execute
On lawless men; preserve from their pursuit.
Thy oft-tried mercy ever is at hand:
Thy judgments on eternal bases stand.

PART XX.
RESCH.

Behold my sorrows, patronise my cause.
Thy Word perform to him that keeps Thy laws.
Death shall devour who Thy commands neglect.
Thou, Great in Mercy, my sought life protect.
In all extremes I have Thy will observ'd,
Griev'd when transgressors from Thy statutes
    swerv'd.
To me, who love Thy laws, Thy grace extend.
Thy truth began with time, and knows no end.

PART XXI.
SCHIN.

Tyrants oppress: Thy Word restrains my mind,
Wherein I joy, like those who treasure find.
Fraud I abhor, enamour'd on Thy ways.
Sev'n times a day my lips Thy justice praise.
Who love Thy laws, sweet peace and safety bless.
In Thee I hope, nor Thy just Will transgress.
Thy Word observe; Thy Statutes I affect,
Which through these human seas my course
    direct.

PART XXII.
TAU.

Accept my pray'rs: with knowledge, Lord, endue;
From death redeem, since to Thy promise true.

Thy statutes taught, I will Thy praise resound,
Thy Word extoll, and laws with justice crown'd:
These are my choice : uphold with Thy right Hand
Who feed on hope, and joy in Thy command.
Prolong my life, that I Thy praise may sing.
Lord, Thy stray'd sheep back to Thy pasture bring.

PSALM CXX.

Tune 5.

ISTRESS'D, and in my mind dismay'd,
When destitute of human aid,
To Thee successfully I pray'd.

Lord, shield me from the fraudulent,
From those that are on malice bent,
Who envious calumnies invent.

O thou false tongue, steep'd in the gall
Of serpents ! what reward for all
Thy mischief shall to thee befall?

Like arrows shot from Parthian strings,
Fir'd juniper, and scorpions' stings,
Such art thou, O thou worst of things!

Woe's me, that I from Israel
Exiléd, must in Mesech dwell,
And in the tents of Ismael!

O how long shall I live with those
Whose savage minds sweet peace oppose,
Where fury by dissuasion grows?

PSALM CXXI.

Tune 13.

O the hills thine eyes erect,
Help from those alone expect.
He, Who heav'n and earth hath made,
Shall from Sion send thee aid.
God, thy ever watchful guide,
Will not suffer thee to slide.
He, ev'n He, Who Israel keeps,
Never slumbers, never sleeps.
He, thy guard, with wings display'd,
Shall refresh Thee in their shade.
Suns shall not with heat infect,
But their temp'rate beams reflect;
Nor unwholesome serene shall
From the moon's moist influence fall.
When thou travell'st on the way,
When at home thou spend'st the day,
When sweet peace thy life delights,
When embroil'd in bloody fights,
God shall all thy steps attend,
Now and evermore defend.

PSALM CXXII.

Tune 23

HAPPY summons! to the court
And temple of the Lord resort.
Jerusalem, our feet shall tread
Within thy walls! O Thou, the head

Of all the earth and Judah's throne,
Three cities strongly join'd in one!
The tribes in throngs to thee ascend,
The tribes which on the Lord depend.
Fat off'rings to His altar bring,
And His immortal praises sing.
There shall He His tribunal place,
The judgment-seat of David's race.
Your joys shall with your days increase,
Who love and pray for Salem's peace.
May peace within thy walls abound,
Thy palaces with joy resound.
Ev'n for my friend's and kindred's sake,
May never war thy bulwarks shake;
Ev'n for the hope of Israel,
And house where God vouchsafes to dwell.

PSALM CXXIII.

Tune 18.

THOU Mover of the rolling spheres,
I, through the glasses of my tears,
    To Thee my eyes erect:
As servants mark the master's hands,
As maids their mistress's commands,
    And liberty expect;

So we, depress'd by enemies,
And growing troubles, fix our eyes
    On God, Who sits on high;
Till He in mercy shall descend
To give our miseries an end,
    And turn our tears to joy.

O save us, Lord, by all forlorn,
The subject of contempt and scorn,

Defend us from their pride,
Who live in fluency and ease,
Who with our woes their malice please,
And miseries deride.

PSALM CXXIV.

Tune 22.

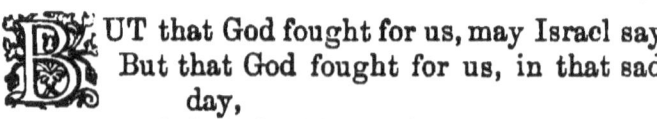UT that God fought for us, may Israel say,
But that God fought for us, in that sad day,
When men inflam'd with wrath against us rose,
We had alive been swallow'd by our foes.
Then had we sunk beneath the roaring waves,
And in their horrid entrails found our graves;
Then had their violence, like torrents pour'd
From melting hills, our wretched lives devour'd.
O blest be God! Who hath not giv'n our blood
To quench their thirst, nor made our flesh their food.
Our souls, like birds, have scap'd the fowler's net;
The snares are broke which for our lives were set:
Our only confidence is in His Name,
Who made the earth, and heav'n's immortal frame.

PSALM CXXV.

Tune 8.

THEY who the Lord their fortress make
Shall like the tow'rs of Sion rise,
Which dreadful earthquakes never shake,
Nor raging tumults of the skies.
Lo! as the hills of Solyma
Divine Jerusalem enclose,

So shall His angels, in the day
  Of danger, shield them from their foes.
The wicked shall not long subject
  Their holy race, lest through despair
They should the laws of God neglect,
  And be as their commanders are.
Lord, to the good be good; the just
  Protect; their punishments increase
Who follow their rebellious lust ;
  But crown Thy Israel with peace.

PSALM CXXVI.

Tune 23.

WHEN God had our deliv'rance wrought,
And Sion out of bondage brought,
It seem'd to us a dream, who were
Distracted between hope and fear.
Then sacred joy fill'd every breast,
In flowing mirth and songs express'd.
The wond'ring heathen oft would say,
How good ! how great a God have they !
Great things for us the Lord hath wrought,
Above the reach of human thought.
We therefore will His praises sing.
The remnant, Lord, from bondage bring,
As rivers through the parched sand,
Or show'rs which fall on thirsty land.
Who sow in tears shall reap in joy.
We, after long captivity,
Unto our native soil retire,
The scope and crown of our desire.

PSALM CXXVII.

Tune 6.

UNLESS the Lord the house sustain,
    They build in vain.
In vain they watch, unless the Lord
    The city guard.
In vain you rise before the light,
And break the slumbers of the night.

In vain the bread of sorrow eat,
    Got by your sweat,
Unless the Lord with good success
    Your labours bless.
For He all good on His bestows,
And crowns their eyes with sweet repose.

Increasing sons, His heritage,
    Renew their age;
The pledges of their fruitful love,
    Giv'n from above:
As formidable to the foe,
As arrows from a giant's bow.

He is belov'd of God, and blest
    Above the rest,
Whose quivers with such shafts abound;
    By men renown'd:
Nor shall his adversary dread,
When they at the tribunal plead.

PSALM CXXVIII.
Tune 13.

HAPPY he who God obeys,
Nor from His direction strays.
Thou shalt of thy labours feed;
All shall to thy wish succeed.
Like a fair and fruitful vine,
By thy house, thy wife shall join.
Sons, obedient to command,
Shall about thy table stand,
Like green plants of olives, set
By the moist'ning rivulet.
He who fears the Pow'r above,
Thus shall prosper in His love.
God shall thee from Sion bless;
Thou shalt joy in the success
Which the Lord will Salem give,
While thou hast a day to live.
Thou shalt see our Israel's peace,
And thy children's large increase.

PSALM CXXIX.
Tune 23.

OFT from my early youth have they
Afflicted me, may Israel say,
Oft from my early youth assail'd;
As oft have their endeavours fail'd.
My back with long deep furrows wound,
As plough-shares ear[1] the patient ground.
The Ever-just hath broke their bands,
And sav'd me from their cruel hands.

---

[1] *Ear*, i. e. plough. In line 14, *comes to ear*.

Let Sion's foes with infamy
Be clothéd, and untimely die:
Be they like corn on houses' tops,
Which reaper's sickle never crops,
Nor binder in his bosom bears,
But withers still before it ears.
No traveller their labours bless,
Nor say, We wish you good success.

PSALM CXXX.

Tune 9.

OUT of the horrors of the deep,
Where fear and sorrow never sleep,
  To Thee my cries
  In sighs arise:
Lord, from despair Thy servant keep:
  O lend a gracious ear,
  And my petitions hear.

For if Thou should'st our sins observe,
And punish us as we deserve,
  Not one of all
  But then must fall,
Since all from their obedience swerve:
  Yet art not Thou severe,
  That we Thy Name might fear.

Thy mercies our misdeeds transcend:
My hopes upon Thy truth depend:
  Disconsolate
  On Thee I wait;
As weary sentinels attend
  The cheerful morn's uprise
  With long-expecting eyes.

O you that are of Jacob's race,
In Him your hopes and comforts place;
 His praises sing,
 The living Spring
Of mercy and redundant grace;
 For He will Israél
Redeem from sin and hell.

PSALM CXXXI.
Tune 17.

THOU, Lord, my Witness art,
I am not proud of heart,
Nor look with lofty eyes,
None envy, nor despise,
Nor to vain pomp apply
My thoughts, nor soar too high;
But in behaviour mild,
And, as a tender child.
Wean'd from his mother's breast,
On Thee alone I rest.
O Israél, adore
The Lord for evermore:
Be He the only scope
Of thy unfainting hope.

PSALM CXXXII.
Tune 22.

REMEMBER David, Lord; remember Thou
His troubles, Thy redemptions, and the vow
He to the Mighty God of Jacob made,
Bound by an oath, and in these words convey'd:

No roof shall cover me, nor sweet repose
Refresh my limbs, or sleep my eyelids close,
'Till I have found a place for His abode,
Ev'n for the temple of the Living God.
The ark, we heard, in Ephrata long stood,
And found it in the valley cloth'd with wood.
We will into Thy tabernacle go,
And there ourselves before Thy footstool throw.
Ascend to Thy eternal rest at length,
Thou, and the Ark of Thy admiréd strength.
O let Thy priests be cloth'd with sanctity,
And all Thy saints sing with triumphant joy.
For David's sake, receive into Thy grace;
From Thy anointed never turn Thy Face.
For thus Thou swor'st Who never wilt forget;
Thy son shall long possess thy royal seat,
And if thy children My commands observe,
Nor from the rules of My prescription swerve,
Their offspring shall the Hebrew sceptre sway,
Ev'n while the sun illuminates the day.
For Sion I have chosen; Sion great
In My affections; My eternal seat.
I will abundantly increase her store,
And with the flow'r of wheat sustain her poor.
Her priests shall blessings to her people bring,
Her joyful saints in sacred measures sing.
There shall the horn of David freshly sprout,
Their lamp of glory never shall burn out.
His diadem shall flourish on his head,
But nets of shame his foes shall over-spread.

THE PSALMS OF DAVID. 289

PSALM CXXXIII.
Tune 23.

BLEST estate! blest from above!
When brethren join in mutual love.
'Tis like the precious odours shed
On consecrated Aaron's head,
Which trickled from his beard and breast,
Down to the borders of his vest.
'Tis like the pearls of dew that drop
On Hermon's ever-fragrant top;
Or which the smiling heav'ns distill
On happy Sion's sacred hill.
For God hath there His favours plac'd,
And joy, which shall for ever last.

PSALM CXXXIV.
Tune 21.

YOU, who the Lord adore,
  And at His altar wait,
Who keep your watch before
  The threshold of His gate,
    His praises sing
    By silent night,
    Till cheerful light
    In th' orient spring.

Your hands devoutly raise
  To His divine recess;
The world's Creator praise,
  And thus the people bless;

U

The God of love,
From Sion's tow'rs,
To you and yours
Propitious prove.

PSALM CXXXV.

PART I. *Tune* 22.

 YOU, who ephods wear and incense fling
On sacred flames, Jehovah's praises sing.
You who His temple guard, O celebrate
His glorious Name, His noble acts relate.
How great a joy with such sincere delight
To crown the day and entertain the night !
For Israel is His choice; and Jacob's race
His treasure, and the object of His grace.
In pow'r how infinite ! how much before
Those mortal gods whom frantic men adore !
All on His will depend; all homage owe,
In heav'n, in earth, and in the depths below.
At His command exhaléd vapours rise,
And in condenséd clouds obscure the skies ;
From thence in show'rs He horrid lightning
    flings,
And from their caves the struggling tempests
    brings.
He the firstborn of men and cattle slew ;
Fresh streams of blood the towns and plains
    imbrew.
Th' inhabitants that drink of Nilus' flood,
At His confounding wonders trembling stood.

PART II.

Great princes, who excell'd in fortitude,
And mighty nations by His pow'r subdu'd.
Strong Sihon, whom the Amorites obey'd;
And strenuous Og, who Bashan's sceptre sway'd;
With all the kingdoms of the Canaanites,
Who to the conquerors resign their rights.
To whom He their dismantled cities grants,
And in those fruitful fields His Hebrews plants.
Thy Name shall last unto eternity,
And Thy immortal fame shall never die.
Thou dost Thy servant pardon and protect,
Advance the humble, and the proud deject.
Those helpless gods, ador'd in foreign lands,
Are gold and silver, wrought by human hands.
Blind eyes have they, deaf ears, still silent tongues;
Nor breath exhale from their inactive lungs.
Who made, resemble them; and such are those
Who in such senseless stocks their hopes repose.
O praise the Lord, ye who from Israel spring;
His praises, O you sons of Aaron, sing;
You of the house of Levi praise His Name;
All you who God adore His praise proclaim.
From Sion praise the only Good and Great,
Who in Jerusalem hath fix'd His seat.

PSALM CXXXVI.

Tune 24.

THE bounty of Jehovah praise :
This God of gods all sceptres sways.
Thanks to the Lord
Of lords afford;

And His amazing wonders blaze.
>> For from the King of kings
>> Eternal mercy springs.

Him praise Who fram'd the archéd sky,
Those orbs that move so orderly.
>> Firm earth above,
>> The floods that move
Display'd, and rais'd the hills on high.
>> For from the King of kings
>> Eternal mercy springs.

Who sun and moon inform'd with light,
To guide the day, and rule the night:
>> The fixéd stars,
>> And wanderers,
Created by Divine foresight.
>> For from the King of kings
>> Eternal mercy springs.

The firstborn of Egyptians slew,
Whose wounds the thirsty earth imbrew;
>> And from that land,
>> With pow'rful Hand,
Th' oppresséd sons of Jacob drew.
>> For from the King of kings
>> Eternal mercy springs.

The parted seas before them fled,
Who in their empty channels tread;
>> The joining waves,
>> Egyptian graves;
And His through foodless deserts led.
>> For from the King of kings
>> Eternal mercy springs.

Who num'rous armies put to flight,
And mighty princes slew in fight:

Og prostrate laid,
Who Bashan sway'd;
And Sihon the crown'd Amorite.
    For from the King of kings
    Eternal mercy springs.

By His strong Hand those giants fell,
And gave their lands to Israel;
    Confirm'd by deed
    Unto their seed,
Who in their conquer'd cities dwell.
    For from the King of kings
    Eternal mercy springs.

Remember'd us in our distress,
And freed from those who did oppress:
    He food doth give
    To all that live.
The God of heav'n, O Israel, bless.
    For from the King of kings
    Eternal mercy springs.

PSALM CXXXVII.

Tune 1.

AS on Euphrates' shady banks we lay,
    And there, O Sion, to thy ashes pay
    Our funeral tears; our silent harps, unstrung,
And unregarded on the willows hung.
Lo, they who had thy desolation wrought,
And captiv'd Judah unto Babel brought,
Deride the tears which from our sorrows spring,
And say in scorn, A song of Sion sing.

A PARAPHRASE UPON

Shall we profane our harps at their command,
Or holy hymns sing in a foreign land?
O Solyma! thou that art now become
A heap of stones, and to thyself a tomb!
When I forget thee, my dear mother, let
My fingers their melodious skill forget:
When I a joy disjoin'd from thine receive,
Then may my tongue unto my palate cleave.
Remember Edom, Lord, their cruel pride,
Who in the sack of wretched Salem cried :—
Down with their buildings, raze them to the ground,
Nor let one stone be on another found.
Thou Babylon, whose tow'rs now touch the sky,
That shortly shalt as low in ruins lie,
O happy! O thrice happy they who shall
With equal cruelty revenge our fall!
That dash thy children's brains against the stones,
And without pity hear their dying groans.

PSALM CXXXVIII.
Tune 20.

Y soul, applaud our glorious King,
Before the gods His praises sing:
His mercy an eternal spring.

For this, on consecrated ground
Will I adore; Thy truth resound;
Thy Word above all names renown'd.

Thou heard'st me when to Thee I cried,
When danger charg'd on ev'ry side,
By Thee confirm'd and fortified.

All those who awful sceptres bear,
When they of Thy performance hear,
Shall worship Thee with reverend fear.

They shall His truth and mercy praise,
Who all the world with justice sways,
Whose wonders adoration raise.

Although enthron'd above the skies,
He on the lowly casts His eyes,
But doth the insolent despise.

Though storms of troubles me enclose,
Yet Thou shalt save me from my foes,
And raise me in their overthrows.

For God His promise will effect,
The faithful faithfully protect,
Nor ever His own choice reject.

PSALM CXXXIX.

PART I.   *Tune 23.*

THOU know'st me, O Thou only Wise,
Seest when I sit, and when I rise;
Canst my concealéd thoughts disclose,
Observ'st my labours and repose;
Know'st all my counsels, all my deeds,
Each word which from my tongue proceeds.
Behind, before, by Thee enclos'd,
Thy Hand on ev'ry part impos'd.
Such knowledge my capacity
Transcends, so wonderful, so high!
O which way shall I take my flight,
Or where conceal me from Thy sight?
Ascend I heav'n, heav'n is Thy Throne;
Dive I to hell, there art Thou known.
Should I the morning's wings obtain,
And fly beyond th' Hesperian main,

Thy pow'rful Arm would reach me there,
Reduce, and curb me with Thy fear.
Were I involv'd in shades of night,
That darkness would convert to light.
What clouds can from discov'ry free?
What night, wherein Thou canst not see?
The night would shine like day's clear flame,
Darkness and light to Thee the same.
Thou sift'st my reins, ev'n thoughts to come;
Thou cloth'dst me in my mother's womb.
Great God, that hath so strangely rais'd
This fabric, be Thou ever prais'd.

Part II.

O full of admiratión
Are these Thy works! to me well-known.
My bones were to Thy view display'd,
When I in secret shades was made;
When wrought by Thee with curious art,
As in the earth's inferior part.
On me, an embryon, didst Thou look;
My members written in Thy book
Before they were; which perfect grew
In time, and open to the view.
Thy counsels admirable are,
And yet as infinite as rare.
O could I number them, far more
Than sands upon the murmuring shore!
When I awake, Thy works again
My thoughts with wonder entertain.
The wicked Thou wilt surely kill.
Hence you, who blood with pleasure spill.
Their tongues Thy Majesty profane,
They take Thy Sacred Name in vain.

Lord, hate not I Thy enemies,
And grieve when they against Thee rise?
I hate them with a perfect hate,
And as my foes would ruinate.
Search and explore my heart: O try
My thoughts and their integrity.
Behold if I from virtue stray,
And lead in Thy eternal way.

PSALM CXL.

Tune 12.

LORD, save me from the violent,
  From him who takes delight in ill,
  Whose heart deceit and mischief fill,
On bloody war and outrage bent.

Their wounding tongues like serpents whet,
  Poison of asps their lips enclose.
  O save from fierce and wicked foes,
Who toils to overthrow me set!

The proud have hid their cords and snares,
  Spread all their nets, their gins have laid.
  To God, Thou art my God, I said,
O gently hear Thy suppliant's pray'rs.

My strong Preserver in the fight,
  As with a helm, my head defends.
  Let not the wicked gain their ends,
Lord, lest their pride rise with their might.

Themselves let their own slanders wound,
  Destroy him who their fury leads.
  Let burning coals fall on their heads,
And quenchless flames embrace them round.

Cast them into the depths below,
   From thence, O never let them rise!
   Let death the slanderer surprise,
And mischief savage wrath o'erthrow.

God to th' afflicted aid will give,
   The poor defend from death and shame.
   The just shall celebrate Thy Name,
And ever in Thy presence live.

PSALM CXLI.

Tune 14.

O Thee I cry: Lord, hear my cries!
   O come with speed unto my aid.
   Let my sad pray'rs before Thee rise,
Like incense on the altar laid;
Or as when I, with hands display'd,
Present my ev'ning sacrifice.

Before my mouth a guardian set,
   My lips with bars of silence close.
O let me not Thy laws forget,
   And wickedly combine with those
   Who Thee and all that's good oppose,
Nor of their deadly dainties Eat.

But let the just wound and reprove;
   Such stripes and checks, an argument
Of their sincere and prudent love;
   Like odours of a fragrant scent,
   Pour'd on my head, no breaches rent:
My pray'rs shall for their safety move.

'Mongst rocks their chiefs in ambush lie,
   Yet have my suff'rings understood.

Our sever'd bones are scatter'd by
  The mouths of graves, like clefts of wood.
  Lord, save from those that hunt for blood:
On Thee with faith I cast mine eye.

O from their machinations free,
  That would my guiltless soul betray;
From those who in my wrongs agree,
  And for my life their engines lay.
  May they by their own craft decay,
But let me Thy salvation see.

PSALM CXLII.

Tune 4.

WITH sighs and cries to God I pray'd,
  To Him my supplication made;
    Pour'd out my tears,
    My cares and fears;
  My wrongs before Him laid.

My fainting spirits almost spent,
He knew the path in which I went.
    Yet in my way
    Their snares they lay,
  With merciless intent.

My eyes I round about me throw,
None see that will th' oppressed know;
    No refuge left,
    Of hope bereft,
  Vain pity none bestow.

Then unto God I cried and said,
Thou art my hope and only aid;

The portión
I build upon,
While with frail flesh array'd.

O Source of mercy, hear my cry,
Lest I with wasting sorrow die:
Shield from my foes,
Who now inclose,
Since of more strength than I.

My soul out of this prison bring,
That I may praise Thee, O my King.
Who trust in Thee
Shall compass me,
And of Thy bounty sing.

PSALM CXLIII.

PART I.   *Tune* 19.

LORD, to my cries afford an ear,
Th' afflicted hear;
According to Thy equity
And truth reply;
Nor prove severe; for in Thy sight
None living shall be found upright.

The foe my soul besiegeth round,
Strikes to the ground;
In darkness hath envelopéd,
Like men long dead;
My mind with sorrow overthrown,
My heart within me stupid grown.

I call to mind those ancient days
Fill'd with Thy praise;

Thy works alone possess my thought,
    With wonder wrought.
To Thee I stretch my zealous hand,
Desir'd like rain by thirsty land.

PART II.

Approach with speed; my spirits fail;
    Thy Face unveil:
Lest I forthwith grow like to those,
    Whom graves inclose.
O let me of Thy mercy hear,
Before the morning sun appear.

My God, Thou art the only scope
    Of all my hope:
O shew me Thy prescribéd way,
    Lest I should stray.
For to Thy throne I raise mine eyes,
My soul, and all my faculties.

Save from my foes; to Thee lo I
    For refuge fly:
Inform me, that I may fulfill
    Thy Sacred Will.
My God, let Thy Good Spirit lead,
That in Thy paths my feet may tread.

O for Thy honour quicken me,
    Who trust in Thee:
Out of these straits, for justice' sake,
    Thy servant take.
In mercy cut Thou off my foes,
Whose hate hath multiplied my woes.

PSALM CXLIV.

PART I. *Tune 23.*

THE Lord, my Strength, be only prais'd,
The Lord, Who hath my courage rais'd,
In doubtful battle giv'n me might,
And skill how to direct and fight.
My Fautor, Fortress, high-built Tow'r;
My Rock, Redeemer, Shield and Pow'r;
My only Confidence, Who still
Subjects my people to my will.
Lord, what is man, or his frail race,
That Thou should'st such a vapour grace?
Man nothing is but vanity,
A shadow swiftly gliding by.
Great God, stoop from the bending skies,
The mountains touch, and clouds shall rise.
From thence Thy wingéd lightning throw,
Rout and confound the flying foe.
Stretch down Thy Hand, which only saves,
And snatch me from the furious waves.
Free from rebellious enemies,
Inur'd to perjuries and lies,
Their hands defil'd with fraud and wrong.
Then will I, in a new-made song,
Unto the softly warbling string,
Of Thy illustrious praises sing.

PART II.

Thou kings preserv'st, hast me preserv'd,
Ev'n David, who Thy will observ'd.
Free from rebellious enemies,
Inur'd to perjuries and lies;

Foul deeds their violent hands defile,
Hands prone to treachery and guile.
That in their youth our sons may grow
Like laurel groves; our daughters show
Like polish'd pillars deck'd with gold,
Which high and royal roofs uphold;
Our magazines abound with grain,
Provision of all sorts contain;
Increasing flocks our pastures fill,
And well-fed steers the fallows till;
That no incursions peace affright,
No armies join in dreadful fight;
No daring foe our walls invest,
Nor fearful shrieks disturb our rest.
Blest people! who in this estate
Enjoy yourselves without debate:
And happy, O thrice happy they,
Who for their God, the Lord obey!

PSALM CXLV.

PART I.   *Tune* 23.

I STILL will of Thy Glory sing,
Thy Name extoll, my God, my King.
No day shall pass without Thy praise,
Prais'd while the sun his beams displays.
Great is the Lord, Whose praise exceeds:
Inscrutable are all His deeds.
One age shall to another tell
Thy works, which so in pow'r excell.
The beauty of Thy excellence
And oracles intrance my sense.

Men shall Thy dreadful acts relate,
My verse Thy greatness celebrate;
To memory Thy favours bring,
And of Thy noble justice sing.
For in Thee grace and pity live,
To anger slow, swift to forgive.
All on Thy goodness, Lord, depend;
Thy mercies all Thy works transcend.
Ev'n all Thy works shall praise Thy Name,
Thy saints shall celebrate the same:
Of Thy far-spreading empire speak,
Thy pow'r, to which all pow'rs are weak:
To make Thy acts to mortals known,
And glory of Thy awful throne.

PART II.

Thy kingdom never shall have end,
Thy rule beyond time's flight extend.
The Lord shall those who fall sustain,
And souls dejected raise again.
All seek from Thee their livelihood,
Thou in due season giv'st them food.
Thy lib'ral Hand men, birds, and beasts,
Ev'n all that live, with plenty feasts.
The Lord is just in all His ways,
Who mercy in His works displays;
Is present by His pow'r with all
Who on His Name sincerely call;
For He will their desires effect,
Regard their cries, from foes protect.
Who love Him, safety shall enjoy:
The Lord the wicked will destroy.
My tongue His goodness shall proclaim.
Mankind for ever praise His Name.

PSALM CXLVI.

HALLELUJAH.   *Tune* 15.

MY soul, praise thou the Lord,
Whilst thou liv'st His praise record.
Whilst I am, Eternal King,
I will of Thy praises sing.
O no hope in princes place,
Trust in none of human race,
Who can give no help at all,
Nor prevent his proper[1] fall.
When his parting breath expires,
He again to earth retires.
Ev'n in that uncertain day
All his thoughts with him decay.
Happy he whom God protects,
He on whom His grace reflects.
Happy he who plants his trust
On the Only Good and Just.
He Who heav'n's blue arch display'd,
He Who earth's foundation laid,
Spread the land-embracing main,
Made whatever all contain.
True to what His word profest,
He revengeth the opprest;
Hungry souls with food sustains,
And unbinds the prisoners' chains.
To the blind restores his sight,
Rears who fall by wicked might.
Righteousness His soul affects.
Friendless strangers He protects,

---

[1] *Proper*, i.e. his own.

Widows and the fatherless ;
Those confounds who these oppress.
Zion, God, thy God shall reign,
While the poles their orbs sustain.
  Hallelujah.

PSALM CXLVII.
Tune 23.

JEHOVAH praise with one consent,
 How comely, sweet, how excellent,
 To sing our Great Creator's praise !
Whose Hands late-ruin'd Salem raise,
Collecting scatter'd Israel,
That they in their own towns may dwell.
He cures the sorrows of our minds,
Our wounds embalms and softly binds.
He numbers heav'n's bright sparkling flames,
And calls them by their sev'ral names.
Great is our God, and Great in Might ;
His knowledge O most infinite !
The humble unto thrones erects,
The insolent to earth dejects.
Present your thanks to our Great King,
On solemn harps His praises sing,
Who heav'n with gloomy vapours hides,
And timely rain for earth provides.
With grass He clothes the pregnant hills,
And hungry beasts with herbage fills.
He seeks the raven's croaking brood
(Left by the old) that cry for food.

PART II.
He cares not for the strength of horse,
Nor man's strong limbs and matchless force ;

But those affects who in His path
Their feet direct with constant faith.
O Solyma, Jehovah praise !
To God thy voice, O Sion, raise !
Who hath thy city fortified,
Thy streets with citizens supplied,
Firm peace in all thy borders set,
And fed thee with the flour of wheat.
He sends forth His commands which fly
More swift than lightning through the sky ;
The snow like wool on mountains spreads,
And hoary frosts like ashes sheds ;
While solid floods their course refrain,
What mortal can His cold sustain ?
At His command, by wind and sun
Dissolv'd th' unfetter'd rivers run.
His laws to Jacob He hath shown,
His judgments are to Israel known.
Not so with other nations deals,
From whom His statutes He conceals.

PSALM CXLVIII.

HALLELUJAH. *Tune 15*

YOU who dwell above the skies,
Free from human miseries,
You whom highest Heav'n embow'rs,
Praise the Lord with all your pow'rs.
Angels, your clear voices raise ;
Him, you heav'nly armies, praise.
Sun and moon, with borrow'd light,
All you sparkling eyes of night,
Waters hanging in the air,
Heav'n of heav'ns, His praise declare.

His deservéd praise record;
His, Who made you by His Word;
Made you evermore to last,
Set your bounds not to be past.
Let the earth His praise resound,
Monstrous whales, and seas profound,
Vapours, lightning, hail and snow,
Storms which when He bids them blow,
Flow'ry hills and mountains high,
Cedars neighbours to the sky,
Trees that fruit in season yield,
All the cattle of the field,
Savage beasts, all creeping things,
All that cut the air with wings.
You who awful sceptres sway,
You inuréd to obey,
Princes, judges of the earth,
All of high and humble birth,
Youths and virgins flourishing
In the beauty of your spring,
You who bow with age's weight,
You who were but born of late,
Praise His Name with one consent:
O how great! how excellent!
Than the earth profounder far,
Higher than the highest star.
He will His to honour raise.
You, His saints, resound His praise,
You who are of Jacob's race,
And united to His grace.
    Hallelujah.

PSALM CXLIX.

Tune 15.

TO the God Whom we adore,
Sing a song unsung before.
His immortal praise rehearse,
Where His holy saints converse.
Israel, O thou His choice,
In thy Maker's praise rejoice.
Zion's sons, rejoice and sing
To the honour of your King.
In the dance His praise resound,
Strike the harp, let timbrels sound.
God, in goodness infinite,
In His people takes delight.
God with safety will adorn
Those whom men afflict with scorn.
Let His saints in glory joy,
Sing as in their beds they lie;
Highly praise the Living Lord,
Arm'd with their two-edged sword,
All the heathen to confound,
And the nations bord'ring round;
Binding all their kings with cords,
Fettering their captive lords,
That they in divine pursuit
May His judgments execute.
As 'tis writ, Such honour shall
Unto all His saints befall.
    Hallelujah.

PSALM CL.

HALLELUJAH.   *Tune* 15.

PRAISE the Lord, enthron'd on high,
Praise Him in His sanctity.
Praise Him for His mighty deeds,
Praise Him Who in pow'r exceeds.
Praise with trumpets, pierce the skies,
Praise with harps and psalteries.
Praise with timbrels, organs, flutes,
Praise with violins and lutes.
Praise with silver cymbals sing,
Praise on those which loudly ring.
Angels, all of human birth,
Praise the Lord of heav'n and earth.
Hallelujah.

THE END OF THE PSALMS OF DAVID.

A PARAPHRASE UPON ECCLESIASTES.

A PARAPHRASE UPON ECCLESIASTES.

CHAPTER I.

HIS Sermon the much-knowing
  Preacher made,
King David's son, who Judah's
  sceptre sway'd.
O restless vanity of vanities!
All is but vanity, the Preacher cries.
What profit have we by our labours won,
Of all beneath the circuit of the sun?
The earth is fix'd, we fleeting: as one age
Departs, another enters on the stage.
The setting sun resigns his throne to night,
Then hastens to restore the morning light.
The wind flies to the south, shifts to the north,
And wheels about to where it first brake forth.
All rivers run into th' insatiate main,
From thence to their old fountains creep again.
Incessantly all toil. The searching mind,
The eye and ear, no satisfaction find.
What is, hath been; what hath been shall ensue;
And nothing underneath the sun is new.

314 A PARAPHRASE UPON

Of what can it be truly said, behold
This never was ? The same hath been of old.
For former ages we remember not,
And what is now will be in time forgot.
Lo I, the Preacher, king of Israel,
Who in ability and pow'r excel,
In wisdom's search applied my industry,
To know whatever was beneath the sky.
(For God this toil on man's ambition lays,
To travel in so intricate a maze.)
I all their works have seen: all are but vain,
Conceiv'd with sorrow, and brought forth with
  pain.
The crooked never can be rectified,
Nor the defective number'd or supplied.
Thus in my heart I said : Thou art arriv'd
At honour's height; more wisdom hast achiev'd
Than all that liv'd in Solyma before,
Thy knowledge, judgment, and experience more.
As wisdom, so I folly did pursue,
And madness tried ; these were vexatious too.
Much wisdom great anxieties infest,
And grief of mind by knowledge is increas'd.

CHAPTER II.

 SAID in my own heart, Go on, and prove
What mirth can do: taste the delights
of love.
In pleasure's change thy careless hours employ :
This also was a false and empty joy.
Avaunt, said I, O laughter, thou art mad !
Vain mirth, what canst thou to contentment add?

Then sought the cares of study to decline
With lib'ral feasts, and flowing bowls of wine.
With all my wisdom exercis'd, to try
If she at length with folly could comply;
And to discover that beatitude
Which mortals all their lives so much pursu'd.
Great works I finish'd, sumptuous houses built,
My cedar roofs with gold of Ophir gilt;
Choice vineyards planted; paradises made,
Stor'd with all sorts of fruits, with trees of shade,
And water'd with cool rivulets, that drill'd
Along the borders: these my fish-pools fill'd.
For service and delight I purchaséd
Both men and maids: more in my house were bred.
My flocks and herds abundantly increas'd;
So great, as never king before possess'd.
Silver and gold, the treasure of the seas,
Of kings, and provinces, foment mine ease.
Sweet voices, music of all sorts, invite
My curious ears, and feast with their delight.
In greater fluency no mortal reigned;
In height of all, my wisdom I retain'd.
I had the beauties which my eyes admir'd,
Gave to my heart whatever it desir'd;
In my own works rejoic'd: the recompence
Of all my labours was deriv'd from thence.
Then I survey'd all that my hands had done;
My troublesome delights. Beneath the sun
What solid good can man's endeavour find?
All is but vanity and grief of mind.
At length I wisdom ponder'd in my thought;
And madness weigh'd: for folly is distraught.
What man can my untracéd steps pursue,
Or do that act which to the king is new?
Then found, how wisdom folly did excell,
As much as brightest heav'n the shades of hell.

The wise man's eyes are tower'd in his head;
The fool in darkness walks, by error led;
Yet equal miseries on either wait,
And both we see obnoxious to one fate.
Thus in my heart I said: The fool and I
Suffer alike, and must together die:
Why then vex I my brains to grow more wise?
Ev'n this was not the least of vanities.
Both must be swallow'd by oblivion;
What is, will not to after times be known.
The wise and foolish to the earth descend,
And in the grave their various travails end.
For this I hated life, which only feeds
Increasing sorrows: fruitless are our deeds,
And wearisome; man no content can find:
For all is vanity and grief of mind.
I hated all the glory I had won;
My state, my structures, all my hands had done;
Foreseeing how that certain hour would come,
When I must leave them; nor yet know to whom.
Who can divine if prudent or a fool?
Yet He must over all my labours rule,
Of all my wisdom's purchases possess'd.
This vanity was equal with the rest.
I therefore sought to make my heart despair,
To slight the frail success of all my care.
What by integrity, and honest toil,
A wise man gathers, must become his spoil
Who only pleas'd his sense. This is a great
Vexation, and an undiscern'd deceit.
What hath a man for all his industry
And grief of soul sustain'd beneath the sky?
All is but sorrow from the hour of birth,
Till he with age return unto the earth:
'Tis travail, pain; night yields him no repose.
This vanity from our first parents flows.

To eat, to drink, to enjoy what we possess
With freedom, is the greatest happiness
That mortals can attain unto : a good
Deriv'd from God, by men not understood.
Who feasted more than I? who spent his store
More lib'rally? or cheer'd his genius more?
God wisdom gives, gives knowledge and delight,
To those whose hearts are perfect in His sight;
To sinners trouble, who their time employ
To gather what the righteous shall enjoy,
By their own avarice in plenty pin'd.
This is a vanity and grief of mind.

CHAPTER III.

LO all things have their times, by God
    decreed
In nature's changes; all things which
    proceed
From man's intentions under the vast sky.
A time when to be born, a time to die :
A time to plant, to extirp; to kill, to cure :
A time to batter down, a time to immure :
A time of laughter, and a time to turn
Our smiles to tears : a time to dance, to mourn :
To scatter stones, to gather them again :
A time to embrace, embraces to refrain :
A time to get, to lose; to save, to spend :
To tear asunder, and the torn to mend :
A time to speak, from speaking to surcease :
A time for love, for hate; for war, for peace.
What good can human industry obtain,
When all things are so changeable and vain?

For God on man these various labours throws,
To afflict him with variety of woes.
He in their times all beautiful hath made ;
The world into our narrow hearts convey'd :
Yet cannot they the causes apprehend
Of His great works ; the original nor end.
What other good can man from these produce,
But to take pleasure in their present use ?
To eat, to drink, t' enjoy what is our own,
Is such a gift as God bestows alone.
His purpose is eternal ; nor can we
Add or subtract from His Divine decree :
That mortals might their bold attempts forbear,
And curb their wild affections by His fear.
What hath been, is ; what shall be, was before ;
And what is past, the Almighty will restore.
Besides, the seats of justice I survey'd,
There saw how favour and corruption sway'd.
Then said I in my heart, God surely shall
Reward the just; the unjust to judgment call.
All purposes and actions have their times :
A time for vengeance to pursue our crimes.
As much as sense concerns, God manifests
To men how little they dissent from beasts :
One end to both befalls ; to equal death
Are liable, and breathe the self-same breath.
Then what pre-eminence hath man above
A beast ; since both so transitory prove ?
Both travel to one home, are earth, and must
Return to their originary dust.
Who knows that souls of men ascend the sky ?
That those of beasts with their frail bodies die ?
What mortal, then, can make so good a choice,
As in his own acquirements to rejoice ?
This is his portion : for of things to come,
None can inform him in the grave's dark womb.

CHAPTER IV.

WHEN I observ'd the bold oppressions done,
In presence of the all-surveying sun;
Beheld the tears that fell from sorrow's eyes,
No comforter t' assuage her miseries;
With all th' oppressor's pow'rful violence;
While weak integrity found no defence.
For this, before the living I preferr'd
Those whom the quiet caves of death interr'd:
Before them both, such as have yet not been,
Nor these diversities of evil seen.
Again observ'd, how our best actions bred
Ignoble envy, by our virtue fed;
Nor friendship could so great a vice control.
This was a vanity and grief of soul.
The fool sits with his arms across; his hours
In sloth consumes, and his own flesh devours.
Better, saith he, a handful is obtain'd
With happy ease, than two by trouble gain'd.
While I this chase of vanity pursue,
A worse presents her folly to my view:
Lo, one who hath no second, child, or heir,
Wears out his life in restless toil and care,
To gather riches; nor can satisfy,
With all his store, the avarice of his eye;
Nor thinks, for whom do I my soul deceive,
And injur'd nature of her dues bereave?
This is a sore disease, if truly known,
And such a vanity as yields to none.
Two better are than one; of more regard;
Their labour less, and greater their reward.

If either fall, one will the other raise;
When he who walks alone, his life betrays.
If two together lie, both warmth beget;
But he who lies alone receives no heat.
If one prevails, two may that one resist:
Cords hardly break which of three lines consist.
More real worth a poor wise child adorns,
Than an old foolish king who counsel scorns.
He from a prison to a throne ascends:
This, born a prince, his life obscurely ends.
His subjects after his successor run,
As from the setting to the rising sun.
The vulgar are inconstant in their choice,
Nor in the present government rejoice;
The following, as the first, to change inclin'd.
This is a vanity and grief of mind.

CHAPTER V.

HITHER thou goest conceive, and to what end,
When thy bold feet the House of God ascend.
There rather hear His life-directing rules
Than offer up the sacrifice of fools.
For sinful are their gifts who neither know
What they to God should give, or what they owe.
The riot of thy tongue let fear restrain,
Nor with rash orisons His ears profane.
God sits in heav'n, with rays of beauty crown'd;
Thou a poor mortal creep'st upon the ground.
Since nothing lies concealéd from His view,
Nor 'scapes His knowledge, let thy words be few.

As dreams proceed from multitude of cares,
So multitude of words a fool declares.
Perform thy vows to God without delay:
Fools please not Him: thy vows sincerely pay.
Since they are off'rings of the grateful will,
Vow not at all, or else thy vows fulfill.
Let not thy tongue oblige thy flesh to sin,
Nor say, I err'd ; by that pretext to win
Thy angel's pardon. Why should'st thou incense
Thy God, and draw His wrath on thy offence?
In multitudes of words and dreams appear
Like vanities : my son, Jehovah fear.
Nor let it quench thy piety, when thou
Shalt see the poor beneath the mighty bow;
All laws perverted, justice cast aside,
As if the universe had lost her guide;
That Pow'r to Whom all are subordinate,
Shall crush them with an unsuspected fate.
The mother earth to all her bosom yields :
Ev'n princes are beholding to the fields.
Who silver covet and excess of gain,
Shall ever want : this folly is as vain.
As riches multiply, ev'n so do they
Who feed thereon, and on their plenty prey.
What profit to the owner can arise,
But to behold them with his careful eyes?
Sweet is the sleep which honest toil begets,
Whether he liberally, or little eats :
When ever-troublesome abundance keeps
The wealthy waking, and affrights his sleeps.
What penury than riches can be worse,
If by the owner turn'd into a curse?
Or to consuming vice become a spoil?
Who sons begets to misery and toil.
Naked he issu'd from his mother's womb,
And naked must descend into his tomb.

Y

Of all, with travail got, and kept with fear,
He nothing to the house of death shall bear,
But must return as empty as he came,
His entry and his exit but the same.
What boots it then to labour for the wind?
This is a sore affliction to the mind.
He feeds his sorrow in continual night,
Replete with anguish, fury, and despite.
This truth have I found out in her pursuit:
To feed our bodies, to enjoy the fruit
Of our enrich'd endeavours, and to give
Ourselves their comforts, whilst on earth we live,
Is good and pleasurable: this alone
Is all we have that can be call'd our own.
For to have riches, and the pow'r withal
To use them freely, is the principal
Of earthly benefits; for God on those
He most affects this happiness bestows.
That man retains no sense of former ills,
Whose heart the Lord of life with gladness fills.

CHAPTER VI.

THIS, as a common misery, have I
With sorrow seen beneath the ambient
   sky:
God riches and renown to men imparts,
Ev'n all they wish; and yet their narrow hearts
Cannot so great a fluency receive,
But their fruition to a stranger leave.
What falser vanity, or worse disease,
Could ever on the life of mortals seize?
Though he a hundred children should beget,
Though many years should make his age complete,

Yet if he to himself his own deny,
Then want a grave and violently die,
Better were an abortive, born in vain,
That in obscurity departs again,
Envelopéd with shrouds of endless night,
Who never saw the sun display his light,
Nor good or evil knew—he is more blest,
And soon descends to his perpetual rest.
Though th' other twenty ages have surviv'd,
His misery is but the longer liv'd.
Yet both must to that fatal mansion go,
Where they to none are known or any know.
All that man labours for is but to eat,
Yet is his soul not satisfied with meat.
What therefore hath the wise more than the fool?
What wants the poor that can his passions rule?
Far better is a clear and pleas'd aspéct,
Than meagre looks which vast desires detect,
Such as can never satisfaction find :
Yet this is vanity and grief of mind.
For be he what he will, he must be man;
A name replete with misery; nor can
But desp'rately with such a Pow'r contend,
On Whom himself and all the world depend.
As riches, so our cares and fears increase :
O discontented man, where is thy peace?
Who knows what's good for thee in these thy days
Of vanity ? A shadow so decays.
Or can inform thy soul what will befall,
When thou art lost in greedy funeral?

CHAPTER. VII.

AN honest name, acquir'd by virtuous deeds,
The fragrant smell of precious oils exceeds.
Ev'n so the hour of death that of our birth;
Which fame secures, and earth restores to earth.
Better to be at funerals a guest,
Than entertainéd at a nuptial feast.
For all must to the shades of death descend,
And those that live should think of their last end.
Sorrow than mirth more to perfection moves,
For a sad countenance the soul improves.
The wise will therefore join with such as mourn,
But fools into the bowers of laughter turn.
A wise man's reprehensions, though severe,
More than the songs of fools should please the ear.
As thorns beneath a caldron catch the fire,
Blaze with a noise, and suddenly expire,
Such is th' immoderate laughter of vain fools:
This vanity in our distemper rules.
Oppression's purchases the judgment blind,
Make wise men mad: a gift corrupts the mind.
Beginnings in their ends their meed obtain:
Humility more conquers than disdain.
Nor be thou to distracting anger prone:
By her deformities a fool is known.
Nor murmuring say: Why are these days of ours
Worse than the former? Doth the Chief of pow'rs
So diff'rently th' affairs of mortals sway?
Such questions but thy arrogance display.
Wisdom with ancient wealth not got by care,
Great blessings heap on those who breathe this air.
Both are to mortals a protecting shade,
When bitter storms or scorching beams invade:

But if divided, he, who is possest
Of life-infusing wisdom, is more blest.
God's works consider: who can rectify,
Or make that straight which He hath made awry?
In thy prosperity let joy abound,
Nor let adversity thy patience wound;
For these by Him so intermixéd are,
Than no man should presume, nor yet despair.
All perturbations, all things that have been,
I, in my days of vanity, have seen:
How their own justice have the just destroy'd,
And how the vicious have their vice enjoy'd.
Be therefore not too righteous nor too wise,
For why should'st thou thy safety sacrifice?
Be not too wicked nor too foolish; why
Should'st thou by violence untimely die?
'Tis best for thee that thou to neither lean,
But warily observe the safer mean.
For they shall all their miseries transcend,
Who God adore, and on His will depend.
A wise man is by wisdom fortified;
More strong than twenty which the city guide.
For justice is not to be found on earth:
None good, nor innocent, of human birth.
Give not to all that's said an open ear,
Lest thou thy servants' execrations hear;
For thy own heart can tell that thou hast done
The like to others: thy example shun.
All this by wisdom tried, I seeméd wise:
But she from human apprehension flies.
Can that which is so far remov'd, and drown'd
In such profundities, by man be found?
Yet in her search I exercis'd my mind,
Of things the causes and effects to find;
The wickedness of folly sought to know:
Folly and madness from one fountain flow.

More sharp than death I found her subtle art,
Who nets spreads in her eyes, snares in her heart,
Her arms inthralling chains: the prudent shall
Escape; the fool by her enchantments fall.
Of all the Preacher hath experience made ;
The reasons, one by one, distinctly weigh'd :
Yet could I not attain to what I most
Desir'd to know ; in my inquiry lost.
One good among a thousand men have known ;
Among the female sex of all not one.
Though in perfection God did man create,
Yet we through vanity degenerate.

CHAPTER VIII.

IS any equal to the truly wise ?
To him that can interpret mysteries ?
For wisdom makes the face of man to shine
With awful majesty and light divine.
Observe the king's commands: remember thou,
Ev'n in that duty, thy religion's vow.
Depart not discontented, nor dispute
With him who can with punishments confute.
For pow'r is thronéd in the breath of kings,
And who dare say they charge unlawful things ?
He who obeys, destruction shall eschew :
A wise man knows both when and what to do.
For all our purposes on time depend,
And judgment ; to produce them to their end.
They wander in the pensive shades of night,
Who want the guide of this directing light;
Surpris'd by unexpected miseries :
Nor can instruction make the foolish wise.

What guard of teeth can keep our parting breath?
Or who resist the fatal stroke of death?
None shall return with conquest from that field;
Nor vice protection to the vicious yield.
This vanity I saw beneath the sun;
The mighty by abuséd pow'r undone:
And though intomb'd with sumptuous funeral,
In his own city soon forgot by all.
Impiety delights in her misdeeds;
In that revenge so tardily succeeds.
Although a sinner sin a hundred times,
And were his years as num'rous as his crimes,
Yet God to those his mercy will extend,
Whose humble souls are fearful to offend.
But bold transgressors with destruction meet,
Their shorten'd days shall like a shadow fleet.
Among the sons of men this mischief reigns;
Exalted vice the meed of virtue gains:
And those afflictions which to vice are due,
Suppresséd virtue furiously pursue.
Then I commended life-prolonging mirth:
To feed upon the bounty of the earth,
And drink the gen'rous grape's refreshing juice,
Is all the good our labours can produce.
This is the best of life: by God alone
Bestow'd on man; and only is his own.

CHAPTER. IX.

WHEN I aspir'd to know how God th' affairs
Of men dispos'd; observ'd the restless cares,
The travails and disturbéd thoughts, which keep
The toiling brain from the relief of sleep;

I then perceiv'd that human industry
Could not the ways nor works of God descry.
Though men endeavour, though the wise suppose
They apprehend, yet none His wisdom knows;
But this have found; that both the just and wise,
Their industry, ev'n all their faculties,
Are in His rule, and by His motion move,
Nor can determine of His hate or love.
All under heav'n succeeds alike to all;
To good and bad the same events befall;
To pure, impure; to those who sacrifice,
To those who piety and God despise;
To th' innocent, the guilty; such who fear
Flagitious oaths, and those who fearless swear.
What greater mischief rules beneath the sun
Than this; that all unto one period run?
Men, while they live are mad; profanely spend
Their flight of time, then to the dead descend.
Yet those have hope who with the living dwell:
For living dogs dead lions far excell.
The living know that they at length must die:
They nothing know who in earth's entrails lie.
What better times can they expect, who rot
In silent graves, and are by all forgot?
Abolish'd is their envy, love, and hate;
Bereft of all which they possest of late.
Then take my counsel; eat thy bread with joy;
Let wine the sorrows of thy heart destroy.
Why should unfruitful cares our souls molest?
Please thou thy God, and in His favour rest.
Be thy apparel ever fresh and fair;
Pour breathing odours on thy shining hair;
Enjoy the pleasures of thy gentle wife,
Through all the course of thy short-dated life.
For this is all thy industry hath won;
Ev'n all thou canst expect beneath the sun.

Since Time hath wings, what thou intend'st to do,
Do quickly, and with all thy pow'r pursue.
No wisdom, knowledge, wit, or work, will go
Along with thee unto the shades below.
I see the swift-of-foot wins not the race,
Nor wreaths of victory the valiant grace;
The wise, to feed his hunger, wanteth bread;
Riches are not by knowledge purchaséd;
Nor popular suffrages desert advance:
All rul'd by opportunity and chance.
Man knows not his own fate. As birds are ta'en
With trammels, fishes by th' entangling seine,[1]
Ev'n so the sons of men are unawares
Prevented by destruction's secret snares.
This also have I seen beneath the sun,
So full of wonder, and by wisdom done:
A little city, mann'd but by a few,
To which a mighty king his army drew,
Erected bulwarks, and intrench'd it round,
A poor wise man within the walls was found,
Whose wisdom rais'd the siege; but they ingrate
Neglected him who had preserv'd their state.
Then wisdom before strength should be preferr'd,
Yet is, if poor, despis'd, her words unheard.
Men more should listen to her sober rules,
Than to his cries who governs among fools.
Wisdom th' habiliments of war exceeds,
But folly is destroy'd by her own deeds.
Lo, as dead flies with their ill savour spoil
Th' apothecary's aromatic oil,
Ev'n so a little folly damnifies
The dignity and honour of the wise.
A wise man's heart to his right hand inclines;
A fool t' his left, and such are his designs.
His own disorder'd paths his life defame,
His gesture and his looks a fool proclaim.

---

[1] *Seine*—A drag-net.

CHAPTER X.

ALTHOUGH thy ruler frown, yet do not
thou
Resent his anger with a cloudy brow;
Nor with obedience or thy faith dispense;
For yielding pacifies a great offence.
This in a state no small disorder breeds,
Which from the error of the prince proceeds:
When vicious fools in dignity are plac'd,
The rich in worth trod under and disgrac'd.
Oft have I servants seen on horses ride,
The free and noble lackey[1] by their side.
Who snares for others sets therein shall light:
Who breaks a hedge, him shall the serpent bite.
The stones shall bruise him who pulls down a
wall:
Who hews a tree, by his own axe shall fall.
If th' edge be blunt, in vain his strength he
spends;
But Wisdom all directs to their just ends.
If serpents bite before the charm be sung,
What then avails th' enchanter's babbling tongue?
A wise man's words are full of grace and pow'r:
A fool's offending lips himself devour.
His words begin in folly; which extend
To acts of mischief, and in madness end.
He gives his tongue the reins; as if he knew
More than man knows—th' events that must ensue.
Who in the endless maze of error treads,
Nor knows the way which to his purpose leads.
Woe to that land, that miserable land,
Which gasps beneath a child's unstaid command:

---

[1] *Lackey*—Run on foot.

Whose nobles rise by times to perpetrate
Their luxuries ; the ruin of the state.
Happy that land, whose king is nobly born ;
Whose lords with temperance his court adorn.
By sloth's supine neglects the building falls :
The hands of idleness pull down her walls.
Feasts are for laughter made ; wine cheers our hearts :
But sov'reign money all to all imparts.
Curse not thy rulers though with vices fraught,
Not in thy bed-chamber, nor in thy thought;
For birds will bear thy whisp'rings on their wings,
To the wide ears of death-inflicting kings.

CHAPTER XI.

SCATTER thy bread upon the hungry main;
This thou, in tract of time, shalt find again.
Thy alms dispense to many ; yet to more;
Famine or war perhaps may make thee poor.
Be like the clouds in bounty ; which on all
The thirsty earth in show'rs profusely fall.
Like pregnant trees, that shed on ev'ry side
Their riper fruit ; to none that stoop denied.
They shall not sow who for a calm defer,
Nor shall they reap whom gloomy skies deter.
Know'st thou from whence the struggling tempests come,
Or how our bones are fashion'd in the womb ?
Much less His greatness canst comprise, Who made
The globe of earth, and radiant heav'n display'd.

The seed of charity at sunrise sow,
And when he sets into the furrows throw:
Know'st thou if this or that increase shall yield?
Or both with grateful ears invest thy field?
How sweet is light! how pleasant to behold
The mounted sun descend in beams of gold!
Yet, though a man live long, long in delight,
Let him remember that approaching night,
Which shall in endless darkness close his eyes;
Then will he all as vanity despise.
Young man, rejoice; thy heart's desires fulfill;
No other lord acknowledge but thy will;
Thy senses freely feast: yet shalt thou come
To God's tribunal, and receive thy doom.
Decline His wrath, and sin-inflicting pain:
For both the bud and flow'r of youth are vain.
Think of thy Maker in thy better days,
Before the vigour of thy age decays;
Before that sad and tedious time draw nigh,
When thou shalt loathe thy life, and wish to die.
Before th' informing sun, the cheerful light,
The various moon, and ornaments of night,
In vain for thee their shining tapers bear,
Or fretting drops of rain deep furrows wear.
When they shall tremble who the house defend,
And the strong columns which support it bend.
The grinders fail, reducéd to a few,
The watch no objects through their casements
    view;
Those doors shut up that open to the street,
And when th' unarméd guarders softly meet.
The bird of dawning raise thee with his voice,
Nor thou in women or their songs rejoice.
When thou shalt fear the roughness of the way,
When ev'ry pebble shall thy passage stay.
When th' almond-tree his boughs invests with
    white;

The locust stoops : then dead to all delight
Man must at length to his long home descend:
Behold, the mourners at his gates attend.
Advise, before the silver cord grows slack,
Before the golden bowl asunder crack,
Before the pitcher at the fountain leak,
Or wasted wheel besides the cistern break.
Man, made of earth, resolves into the same:
His soul ascends to God, from Whom it came.
O restless vanity of vanities!
All is but vanity, the Preacher cries.
He who was wise, the people knowledge taught;
His lines with well-digested proverbs fraught.
He found out matter to delight the mind,
And ev'ry word he writ by truth was sign'd.
Wise sentences are goads ; nails closely driv'n
By grave instructors : by one pastor giv'n.
And now, my son, be thou admonishéd
By what thou hast already heard and read.
There is of making many books no end;
And studious night th' intentive spirits spend.
Of all the sum : Fear God, His laws obey :
Man's duty; to felicity the way.
For He shall ev'ry work, each secret thing,
Both good and bad, to public judgment bring.

THE END OF ECCLESIASTES.

A PARAPHRASE UPON THE SONG OF SOLOMON.

IMPRIMATUR.

THO. WYKES.

March 31, 1641.

TO THE KING.

SIR,

I PRESUME to invite you to these Sacred Nuptials: the Epithalamium sung by a crowned muse. Never was there pair of so divine a beauty, nor united in such harmonious affections: and infinitely He deserved her love; redeemed at so dear a price, and enriched with so invaluable a dowry.

SIR, Let me find your pardon for thus long continuing to make my alloy current by the impression of your name. Directed by your propitious aspect, have I safely steered between so many rocks; and now, arrived at my last harbour, have broken up my ruinous vessel.

The humblest of your

Majesty's Servants,

GEORGE SANDYS.

TO THE QUEEN.

CHASTE nymph, you who extracted are
From that swift thunderbolt of war;[1]
Whose innocence and meekness prove
An eagle may beget a dove;
In this clear mirror you may find
The image of your own fair mind;
With each attractive excellence,
Which feasts the more refinéd sense;
The crownéd muse from heav'n inspir'd
With such rich beauties hath attir'd
The Sacred Spouse; for what below
The sun could more perfection show?

---

[1] Henrietta Maria, daughter of Henry IVth of France.

A PARAPHRASE UPON THE SONG OF SOLOMON.

CANT. I.

SPONSA.

OIN Thy life-breathing lips to mine;
Thy love excells the joy of wine.
Thy odours, O how redolent!
Attract me with their pleasing scent:
These, sweetly flowing from Thy Name,
Our virgins with desire inflame.
O draw me, my Belov'd, and we
With wingéd feet will follow Thee.
Thy longing spouse at length, Great King,
Into Thy royal chamber bring:
Then shall our souls, entranc'd with joy,
In Thy due praise their zeal employ;
Thy celebrated loves recite,
Which more than crownéd cups delight.
Who truth and sacred justice prize,
To Thee their hearts shall sacrifice.
You daughters of Jerusalem,
You branches of that holy stem,
Though black, in favour I excel,
Black as the tents of Ismael,

Yet graceful, as the burnish'd throne
And ornaments of Solomon.
Despise not my discolour'd look:
This tawny from the sun I took.
My mother's sons envied my worth,
And, swoln with malice, thrust me forth
To keep their vines in heat of day,
While, ah, my own neglected lay.
More lov'd than all of human seed,
O tell me where Thy sheep do feed;
Where rest they, in what grateful shade,
When scorching beams the fields invade?
Why should I stray, and turn to those
Who are but Thy disguiséd foes?

SPONSUS.

 THOU, the fairest of thy kind!
I will inform thy troubled mind.
Follow the way My flock has led,
And in their steps securely tread;
Thy kids feed on the fruitful plains,
Besides the sheep-cotes of our swains.
Thou, love, art like those generous steeds
Which Pharaoh for his chariot breeds,
Trick'd in their rich caparisons.
How shine thy cheeks with sparkling stones,
Which loosely dangle from thine ears!
Thy neck the ocean's treasure wears.
I will a golden zone impart,
Enamelléd with curious art.

THE SONG OF SOLOMON.

SPONSA.

WHILE He the Prince of Bounty feasts,
And entertains His happy guests,
My spikenard shall perfume His hair,
Whose odour fills the ambient air.
All night His Sacred Head shall rest
Between the pillows of my breast.
Not myrrh, new-bleeding from the tree,
So acceptable is to me:
Nor camphire clusters when they blow,
Which in Engedi's vineyard grow.

SPONSUS.

THY beauty, love, allures My sight,
And sheds a firmament of light.
In either eye there sits a dove,
So mild, so full of artless love!

SPONSA.

THOU, my Belov'd, art fairer far;
Thou as the sun, I but a star.
Come, my Delight, our pregnant bed
Is with green buds and violets spread:
Our cedar roofs are richly gilt,
Our galleries of cypress built.

CANT. II.

SPONSUS.

I AM the lily of the vale,
The rose of Sharon's fragrant dale.
Lo, as th' unsullied lily shows
Which in a brake of brambles grows,
My love so darkens all that are
By erring men admir'd for fair.

Sponsa.

LO, as the tree which citrons bears
    Amidst the barren shrubs appears,
    So my Belov'd excells the race
Of man in ev'ry winning grace.
In His desiréd shade I rest,
And with His fruits my palate feast:
He brought me to His magazines,
Replenish'd with refreshing wines:
And over me, a tender maid,
The ensigns of His love display'd.
With flagons O revive my pow'rs,
And strew my bed with fruits and flow'rs,
Whose taste and smell may cordial prove,
For, ah, my soul is sick with love:
Beneath my head Thy left arm place,
And gently with Thy right embrace.

Sponsus.

YOU daughters of Jerusalem,
    You branches of that holy stem,
    I, by the mountain roes, and by
The harts which through the forest fly,
Adjure you that you silence keep,
Nor, till she call, disturb her sleep.

Sponsa.

IS it a dream? or do I hear
    The Voice that so delights mine ear?
    Lo, He o'er hills His steps extends,
And bounding from the cliffs descends:
Now, like a roe, outstrips the wind,
And leaves the breathéd hart behind.

THE SONG OF SOLOMON.

Behold! without my Dearest stays,
And through the lattice darts His rays.
Thus, as His looks, His words invite:
O thou, the crown of my delight.
Arise my love, my fair one rise,
O come, delay our joy envies.
Lo, the sharp winter now is gone,
The threat'ning tempests overblown;
Hark, how the air's musicians sing,
And carol to the flow'ry Spring.
Chaste turtles, hous'd in shady groves,
Now murmur to their faithful loves;
Green figs on sprouting trees appear,
And vines sweet-smelling blossoms bear.
Arise my love, my fair one rise,
O come, delay our joy envies.
O thou, my dove, whom terror locks
Within the crannies of the rocks,
Come forth, now like thyself appear,
And with thy voice delight Mine ear:
Thy voice is music, and thy face
All conquers with resistless grace.
My lov'd companions, for My sake,
These foxes, these young foxes, take,
Who thus our tender grapes destroy,
And in their prosp'rous rapine joy.

   I am my Love's, and He is mine,
So mutually our souls combine!
He, Whose affection words exceeds,
His flock among the lilies feeds.
Return to me, my only Dear,
Stay till the morning star appear;
Stay till night's dusky shadows fly
Before the day's illustrious eye.
Run like a roe, or hart, upon
The lofty hills of Bitheron.

CANT. III.

SPONSA.

STRETCH'D on my restless bed all night,
I vainly sought my soul's Delight.
Then rose, the city search'd: no street,
No angle my unwearied feet
Untracéd left: yet could not find
The only Solace of my mind.
When lo! the watch, who walk the round,
Me in my soul's distemper found;
Of whom, with passion, I inquir'd,
Saw you the Man so much desir'd?
Nor many steps had farther past,
But found my Love, and held Him fast;
Fast held, till I the so-long sought
Had to my mother's mansion brought.
In that adornéd chamber laid,
Of her who gave me life, I said:
You daughters of Jerusalem,
You branches of that holy stem,
I, by the mountain roes, and by
The hinds which through the forest fly,
Adjure you that you silence keep,
Nor, till He call, disturb His sleep.

CHORUS.

WHAT beauty from the desert comes,
Like spires of smoke rais'd from sweet
        gums,
With aromatic powders fraught,
By merchants from Sabæa brought?

SPONSA.

BEHOLD the bed He rests upon,
The royal bed of Solomon.
Twice-thirty soldiers who excel
In valour, sons of Israel,
So dreadful to their enemies,
Their bright swords mounted on their thighs,
His person guard from the affright,
And treasons of concealing night.
King Solomon a chariot made,
Of trees from Lebanon convey'd;
The pillars silver, and the throne
With gold of Indian ophir shone;
With Tyrian purple ceil'd above,
For Sion's daughter pav'd with love.
Come, holy virgins, O come forth,
Behold a spectacle of worth!
Behold the Royal Solomon,
High mounted on his father's throne;
Crown'd with the crown his mother plac'd
On his smooth brows, with gems enchac'd,
At that solemniz'd nuptial feast,
When joy his ravish'd soul possess'd.

CANT. IV.

SPONSUS.

HOW fair art thou, how wondrous fair!
Thy dove-like eyes in shades of hair,
Whose dangling curls appear like flocks
Of climbing goats from Gilead's rocks.
Thy teeth like sheep in their return
From Chison, wash'd and smoothly shorn.

None mark'd for barren, none of all,
But equal twins at once let fall.
Thy lips like threads of scarlet show,
Whence graceful accents sweetly flow.
Thy cheeks like Punic apples are,
Which blush beneath thy flowing hair.
Thy neck like David's armoury,
With polish'd marble rais'd on high,
Whose walls a thousand shields adorn,
By worthies oft in battle borne.
Thy breasts are twins, twins of the roe,
There grazing where the lilies grow.
I to the mountains will retire,
Where bleeding trees perfumes expire,
Until the morning fleck the sky,
And night's repulséd shadows fly.
How beautiful thy looks appear,
In ev'ry part from blemish clear!
My spouse, at length, let us be gone,
Leave we the fragrant Lebanon.
Look down from Amana, look down
From Shenir's top and Hermon's crown,
From hills where dreadful lions rave,
And from the mountain-leopard's cave.
Thou, who My spouse and sister art,
How hast thou ravishéd My heart!
Struck with one glance of thy bright eyes,
One hair of thine in fetters ties!
Thy beauty, sister, is divine;
Thy love, My spouse, more strong than wine.
Thy odours, far more redolent
Than spices from Panchaia sent.
Thy lips drop honey, from below
Thy palate milk and honey flow.
Thy robes a sweeter odour cast
Than Lebanon with cedars grac'd.

My love, by mutual vows assur'd,
A garden is, with strength immur'd;
A crystal fountain, a clear spring,
Shut up and sealéd with my ring;
An orchard stor'd with pleasant fruits,
Pomegranate trees there spread their roots,
Where sweetly-smelling camphire blows,
And never-dying spikenard grows;
Sweet spikenard, crocus newly-blown,
Sweet calamus and cinnamon;
Those trees which sacred incense shed,
The tears of myrrh, and aloes bled
From bitter wounds; with all the rare
Productions which perfume the air.

SPONSA.

THOSE living springs from Thee proceed,
Whose drills our plants with moisture feed;
Like crystal streams which issue from
The fountain-fruitful Lebanon.
You cooler winds blow from the north,
You dropping southern gales break forth,
On this our garden gently blow,
And through the land rich odours throw.
Come Love, come, with a lover's haste,
Our riper fruits and spices taste.

CANT. V.

SPONSUS.

MY spouse, my sister, thou who art
The joy and treasure of My heart,
I to My garden have retir'd,
Reap'd spices which perfumes expir'd,

Sweet gums from trees profusely shed,
On dropping combs of honey fed;
Drunk morning milk with new-press'd wine:
O friends, whom like desires combine,
Eat, drink, drink freely; nor remove,
Till you be all inflam'd with love.

SPONSA.

ALTHOUGH I sleep, my passions wake,
For He Who knock'd thus sadly spake:
My love, My sister, thou more mild
Than galless doves, My undefil'd,
O let Me enter! Night hath shed
Her dew on My uncover'd head,
Which from My drenchéd locks distills,
And with a frozen numbness chills.
Can I assent to Thy request,
Disrob'd and newly laid to rest?
Shall I now clothe myself again,
And feet so lately wash'd distain?
But when I had His hand discern'd
Drawn from the latch, my bowels yearn'd:
I rose, no longer could defer
To unlock the door; when liquid myrrh,
Thence dropping, on my finger fell,
And breath'd an odoriferous smell.
But, ah! when open'd, He was gone;
His grief fetch'd from my heart a groan.
In vain I sought my soul's Belov'd;
I call'd Him, O too far remov'd!
The watch, and those who walk the round,
In this pursuit th' afflicted found;
Smote, wounded, and profanely tore
The sable veil my sorrow wore.

THE SONG OF SOLOMON.

You virgins of fair Solyma,
I charge you, if you meet Him, say
That I, His spouse, am sick for love,
And with your tears soft pity move.

CHORUS.

 THOU of all our sex most fair,
Can none with thy Belov'd compare?
Doth He so much our loves transcend,
That we alone should Him intend?

SPONSA.

O! in His face the blushing rose,
Join'd with the virgin lily, grows.
Among a myriad He appears
The Chief, and beauty's ensign bears.
His head, adorn'd with burnish'd gold,
Which curls of shining hair enfold,
Black as the newly-prunéd crow.[1]
His eyes like doves by fountains show,
Late bathéd in a rivulet
Of milk, alike exactly set.
His cheeks, sweet spice and flow'rs confer:
His lips, like roses dropping myrrh.
His hand the wand'ring eye invites,
Like rings that blaze with chrysolites.
His belly, polish'd ivory,
Where sapphires in blue branches lie.
His legs, like marble pillars, plac'd
On bases with pure gold enchas'd.
His looks, like cedars planted on
The brows of lofty Lebanon.

---

[1] *Newly-prunéd*—newly-preened.

350 A PARAPHRASE UPON

His tongue the ear with music feeds,
And He in ev'ry part exceeds.
You daughters of Jerusalem,
Such is my Friend, my praise's theme.

CANT. VI.

CHORUS.

AIR virgin, parallel'd by none,
O whither's thy Belovéd gone?
Direct our forward zeal, that we
May join in this pursuit with thee.

SPONSA.

BEHOLD, the More-than-life-desir'd
Down to His garden is retir'd;
There gathers flow'rs, feasts in the shade,
On beds of bruised spices laid.
Our mutual flame all flames exceeds:
My Dear among the lilies feeds.

SPONSUS.

NOT regal Tirzah, Israel's
Delight, thy beauty, Love, excels:
Not thou, divine Jerusalem,
That art of all the world the gem;
Nor armies with their ensigns spread,
So threaten with amazing dread.
O turn from me thy wounding eyes!
In ev'ry glance an arrow flies!
Thy dangling hair appears like flocks
Of climbing goats from Gilead's rocks.

Thy teeth, like sheep in their return
From Chison, wash'd and smoothly shorn;
None mark'd for barren, none of all
But equal twins at once let fall.
Thy cheeks like Punic apples are,
Which blush beneath thy flowing hair.
They boast of many queens, great store
Of concubines, and virgins more
Than can be told: My undefil'd
Is all in one; the only child
Of her fair mother; and brought forth
To show the world an unknown worth.
Queens, virgins, concubines, beheld,
Admir'd, and bless'd th' unparallel'd.

Chorus.

WHO'S this, who like the morning shews,
When she her paths with roses strews?
More fair than the replenish'd moon,
More radiant than the sun at noon?
Not armies with their ensigns spread,
So threaten with amazing dread.

Sponsus.

I TO My pleasant gardens went,
Where nutmegs breathe a fragrant scent,
To see the gen'rous fruits which grac'd
The pregnant vale with springs enchac'd;
To see the vines disclose their gems,
And granates blooming on their stems.
Then unaware, and half amaz'd,
Methought My ravish'd soul was rais'd
Up to a chariot, swift as winds,
Drawn by My people's willing minds.

CHORUS.

RETURN, fair Shulamite, return
To us who for thy absence mourn.
What see you in the Shulamite?
Two armies prevalent in fight.

CANT. VII.

SPONSUS.

PRINCESS, thou than life more dear,
How beautiful thy feet appear,
When they, with purple ribands bound,
In golden sandals print the ground!
Thy joints, like jewels, which impart
To wond'ring eyes the workman's art.
Thy navel, like a mazer, fill'd
With juice from rarest fruits distill'd.
Thy belly, like a heap of wheat,
With never fading lilies set.
Thy breasts two roes, new weanéd, show,
Which fell at once from one fair doe.
Thy neck an ivory tow'r displays:
Thine eyes, which shine with equal rays,
Like Heshbon's pools by Bathrabim,
Where silver-scaléd fishes swim.
Thy nose presents that tow'r upon
The face of flow'ry Lebanon,
Which all the pleasant plain surveys,
Where Abana her streams displays.
Thy head, like Carmel, cloth'd with shade,
Whose tresses Tyrian fillets braid.
The king, from cypress galleries,
This chain of strong affection ties.

How pleasant ! O how exquisite !
Thy beauty fram'd for sweet delight!
Thy stature like an upright palm !
Thy breasts like clusters dropping balm!
I will ascend the palm's high crown,
Whose boughs victorious hands renown,
And, from the spreading branches' root,
Will gather her delicious fruit.
Thy breasts shall like ripe clusters swell,
Thy breath like new-pull'd citrons smell.
Choice wines shall from thy palate spring,
Most acceptable to the King,
Which sweetly shall descend, and make
The dumb to speak, the dead to wake.

SPONSA.

MY Belov'd am only Thine,
And Thou by just exchange art mine.
Come, let us tread the pleasant fields,
Taste we what fruit the country yields,
And in the villages repose,
When shades of night all forms inclose :
Then with the early morn repair
To our new vineyard; see if there
The tender vines thrust forth their gems,
And granates blossom on their stems.
There, where no frosts our spring destroy,
Shalt Thou alone my love enjoy.
How sweet a smell our mandrakes yield !
Our gates with various fruits are fill'd,
Fruits that are old, fruits from the tree
New-gather'd, all preserv'd for Thee.

CANT. VIII.

SPONSA.

HAD we from one mother sprung,
Both at her breasts together hung!
Then should I meet Thee in the street,
With unreprovéd kisses greet,
And to my mother's house conduct,
Where Thou Thy sister shouldst instruct.
There would I spicéd wines produce,
And my pomegranates' purple juice;
Thy left arm for my pillow plac'd,
And strictly with Thy right embrac'd.
You virgins, born in Sion's towers,
I charge you, by the Chief of powers,
That you a constant silence keep,
Nor, till He call, disturb His sleep.

CHORUS.

HO'S this, whose feet the hills ascend
From deserts, leaning on her friend?

SPONSA.

MY Belov'd first raiséd thee
From under the pomecitron tree:
Thy careful mother, in that shade,
With anguish her fair belly laid.
Be I, O Thou my better part,
A seal imprest upon Thy heart.

May I Thy finger's signet prove,
For death is not more strong than love;
The grave not so insatiate,
As jealousies inflame debate.
Should falling clouds with floods conspire,
Their waters could not quench love's fire:
Nor all in nature's treasury
The freedom of affection buy.
We have a sister immature,
That hath no breasts, as yet obscure:
What ornaments shall we bestow,
When mortals her endowments know?

SPONSUS.

IN her, if strongly built to bear,
  We will a silver palace rear;
  Or, if a door, to deck the same,
Will leaves of carvéd cedar frame.

SPONSA.

I AM a firm foundation
  For my Belov'd to build upon:
  My breasts are tow'rs; I His delight,
His object and sole favourite.

SPONSUS.

LATE in Baal-Hamon Solomon
  Let forth his vineyard: ev'ry one,
  For fruits and wines there yearly made,
A thousand silver shekels paid.

356 THE SONG OF SOLOMON.

SPONSA.

THIS vineyard, this, which I possess,
   With diligence I daily dress.
   Thou, Solomon, shalt have thy due:
Two hundred more remain for you
(Out of the surplus of our gains)
Who in our vineyard took such pains.

SPONSUS.

THOU, that in the gardens liv'st,
   And life-infusing counsel giv'st
   To those that in thy songs rejoice,
To Me address thy cheerful voice.

SPONSA.

COME, my Belov'd, O come away!
   Love is impatient of delay:
   Run, like a youthful hart, or roe
On hills where precious spices grow.

THE END OF THE SONG OF SOLOMON.

A PARAPHRASE
UPON THE LAMENTATIONS
OF JEREMIAH.

A PARAPHRASE UPON THE LAMENTATIONS OF JEREMIAH.

Chap. I.

HOW like a widow, ah! how desolate
This city sits, thrown from the pride
 of state!
How is this potent queen, who laws
 to all
The neighbouring nations gave, become a thrall!
Who nightly tears from her salt fountains sheds,
Which fall upon her cheeks in liquid beads.
Of all her lovers none regard her woes,
And her perfidious friends increase her foes.
Judah in exile wanders; ah! subdu'd
By vast afflictions and base servitude.
Among the barbarous heathen finds no rest;
At home, abroad, on ev'ry side opprest.
Ah! see how Sion mourns! her gates, and ways,
Lie unfrequented on her solemn days.
Her virgins weep, her priests lament her fall,
And all her sustenance converts to gall.
A wretched vassal to her savage foes:
Her num'rous sins the authors of these woes.

Behold, how they, who by her losses thrive,
Into captivity her children drive!
O Sion's daughter, all thy beauty's lost!
Thy chaséd princes are like harts imbost,
Which find no water, and enfeebled fly
Before the eager hunters' dreadful cry.
Jerusalem, in these her miseries,
And days of mourning, sets before her eyes
Those vanish'd pleasures which she once enjoy'd,
Her people now by hostile swords destroy'd;
Whil'st none afford compassion to her woes,
Her sabbaths scorn'd by her insulting foes.
Jerusalem hath sinn'd, is now remov'd
For her uncleanness: those who lately lov'd,
As much despise; her nakedness descried:
Who sighs for shame, and turns her face aside.
Pollution stains her skirts; yet her last end
Remember'd not: for this without a friend
Stupendously she fell. Great God! behold
My sorrows, since the foe is grown so bold!
Hath ravish'd all wherein she took delight,
His insolence contending with his might!
Ah! she hath seen th' uncircumcis'd profane
Thy temple, whose approach Thy laws restrain.
Her people sighing seek for bread; who give
Their wealth for food, that their faint souls may live.
Consider, Lord! O look on the forlorn!
Who am to all the world a gen'ral scorn.
You passengers, though this concern not you,
Here fix your steps, and my strange suff'rings view.
Was ever sorrow like my sorrow known,
Which God hath on me in His fury thrown?
He from the breaking clouds His flames hath cast,
Which in my bones the boiling marrow waste;
Hath set snares for my feet, thrown to the ground,
Left desolate and fainting with my wound.

Who of my sins hath made a yoke, to check
My insolence, and cast it on my neck.
My strength hath broken, to my enemies
Subdu'd my pow'rs, now ah! too weak to rise.
He, in the midst of me, hath trodden down
My mighty men, and those of most renown.
His troops on my strong youth like torrents rush'd,
As in a wine-press Judah's daughter crush'd.
For this I weep! my eye, my gallèd eye,
Dissolves in streams; for he who should apply
Balm to my wounds, far, O far off is fled!
My children desolate, their foe their head.
Her hands sad Sion rais'd, no comfort found;
Jehovah charg'd her foes to gird her round.
Jerusalem, O thou of late belov'd,
Now like a menstruous woman art remov'd.
The Lord is just; 'tis I that have rebell'd,
And by my wild revolt His grace expell'd.
Hear, and behold my woes! my orphans torn
From my forc'd arms, and into exile borne.
I to my boasting lovers call'd for aid,
But they their vows infring'd, my trust betray'd.
My priests and princes, while they seek for bread
To feed their hungry souls, augment the dead.
Lord, look on me! my heart rolls in my breast,
My bowels toil like seas with storms oppress'd.
I have provok'd Thy vengeance with my sin:
Without the sword destroys, and dearth within.
My sighs no pity move: my cruel foes
Enjoy Thy wrath, and glory in my woes.
Yet that presagèd time will come, when they
Shall equal sorrows to Thy justice pay.
O set their impious deeds before Thine eyes,
And press them with my weighty miseries
(The birth of sin) which break into complaint;
My groans are numberless, my spirits faint.

CHAP. II.

HOW hath Jehovah's wrath, O Sion, spread
A veil of clouds about thy daughter's head!
From heav'n to earth thy beauty, Israel,
   thrown,
Nor in His fierce displeasure spar'd His own!
How hath He swallow'd Judah's mansions! ras'd
His holds, and to the ground his bulwarks cast!
The land in His relentless rage profan'd,
And with the blood of her own princes stain'd!
He in His indignation hath the horn
Of Israel from his bleeding forehead torn.
Before the foe, O forc'd to fly with shame!
His wrath to Jacob a devouring flame.
Foe-like hath bent His bow; His hostile Hand
Advanc'd and slain the beauty of the land,
All that the eye attracted with desire,
And pour'd His anger forth like floods of fire.
Against thee, Solyma, converts His pow'rs;
Sad Israel and his palaces devours,
His strong-built fortresses to ruins turns;
Whilst Judah's daughter for her children mourns.
His tabernacle He with violence
Hath now demolish'd, like a garden fence.
None Sion's feasts and sabbaths celebrate,
Both king and priest obnoxious to His hate.
Detests His sanctuary, and forsakes
His flameless altar; while the enemy takes
His palaces and walls, fill'd with their cries,
As late by us in our solemnities.
The ruin of Jerusalem designs,
And levels the foundation with His lines.
Nor His fierce Hand withdraws: the tott'ring walls
And stooping turrets languish in their falls.

Her gates sink to the earth, with shiver'd bars ;
Her king and princes slaves, or slain in wars.
All laws surcease. Jehovah to her seers
No more by visions or by dreams appears.
Her elders sit on earth with silent woe,
And dust upon their silver tresses throw ;
In sackcloth mourn. Her virgins hang their heads,
Like drooping flow'rs that bow to their cold beds.
My bowels toil, mine eyes with tears are drown'd,
My bleeding liver pour'd upon the ground,
To see my tender babes, unpitied, lie
On flinty pavements, and through famine die ;
While others to their weeping mothers say,
O give us food, our hunger to allay!
Then, fainting by the bloodless wound of death,
In their enfolding arms sigh out their breath.
How shall my tongue express, O how compare,
Thy matchless sorrows, to assuage thy care,
Distresséd Sion's daughter! for thy breach
Is like the seas, whose rage no bounds impeach.
Vain tales and foolish have thy prophets told,
Nor would they thy exiling sins unfold;
False burthens and false prophecies invent,
The fatal authors of thy banishment.
The passengers, they wry their heads aside,
Hiss at thee, clap their hands, and thus deride :
Is this their only joy? which they of all
The world the beauty and perfection call?
Thy foes make mouths, scoff, grind their teeth,
  and say,
Now have we swallow'd our desiréd prey.
This is that day we did so long expect,
Wherein our hopes have had their wish'd effect!
God hath accomplishéd His old decree;
We thy oft-menacéd destruction see;

Hath ruin'd without pity, made a scorn
To thy triumphant foe, and rais'd his horn.
To Him their hearts now cry: O Sion's tow'rs!
All day, all night, let tears descend in show'rs.
O never give thy lab'ring thoughts repose,
Nor let the humid night thy eyelids close!
Arise and cry; cry from the night's first hour;
Thy heart before thy God like water pour.
O raise thy hands to heav'n, lest famine's force
Thy children's souls from their pale corps divorce.
Lord, see Thy massacres! shall cursèd wombs
Become their new-born children's fatal tombs?
Thy priests and prophets by the sword are slain,
And with their blood Thy sanctuary stain.
Lo! in the streets old men and infants lie,
My virgins and bold youth by slaughter die.
Thou with their blood Thy vengeance didst imbrew,
Thy burning fury without pity slew.
As in a solemn day, Thy terrors have
Environ'd me: Thy anger cloys the grave.
Those whom I swaddled, in my bosom bred,
The barbarous foe hath sent unto the dead.

CHAPTER III.

LO, I, the man, who by the wrath of God
Have seen affliction's storms, and felt His
rod!
He hath depriv'd me of the cheerful light,
Envelopèd with shades more dark than night,
Against me His revengeful forces bent;
Nor sets His anger with the sun's descent.
My flesh hath wasted, wrinkled my smooth skin
With sorrow's age, and broke my bones within.

Against me digg'd a trench, cast up a mound,
With travail's bitter gall besieg'd me round.
Imprison'd where no beams their brightness shed,
Like that dark region peopled by the dead.
On ev'ry side my flight with bars restrains,
And clogs my gallèd legs with massy chains.
Who stops His ears against my cries and pray'rs,
With stone immures, and spreads my path with
   snares.
He like a bear or lion lies in wait,
Diverts, in pieces tears, leaves desolate.
At me, as at a mark, His bow He drew,
Whose arrows in my blood their wings imbrew.
He lets the people circle me in throngs,
Who all the day deride with spiteful songs.
With wormwood made me drunk, with gall hath fed,
My teeth with gravel broke, with ashes spread.
My soul to peace is such a stranger grown,
As if I never better days had known.
When I my wrongs to memory recall,
My miseries, my wormwood, and my gall,
My passions thus exclaim: Ah! perishéd
Are all my hopes! from me my strength is fled!
These thoughts my soul have humbled, trod to earth
My pride, and giv'n my hopes a second birth.
'Twas Thy abundant goodness, Lord, that all
Did not together in one ruin fall.
Thy mercies with the rising light renew,
And Thy fidelity, as large as true.
My soul is arm'd with stedfast confidence,
Since Thou my portion art, and strong defence.
To those how gracious who on Thee rely!
Who seek Thee with unfainting industry!
'Tis good to hope and rest upon Thy truth,
'Tis good to bear Thy yoke in early youth.

Alone he silent sits, nor will distrust
Thy promise when he hides his head in dust.
His cheek submits to blows, by all revil'd,
Yet knows at length Thou wilt be reconcil'd.
When God with grief hath fixt thee to the ground,
His mercy will pour balm into thy wound.
For He delights not in our misery,
On those to trample who in fetters lie;
Hates that the weak should be oppress'd by might,
Or justice suffer in the judge's sight.
O tell, what can befall beneath the sun,
That is not by the Lord's appointment done?
Both good and bad from Him proceeds; why then
Grudge you at punishment, vain sinful men?
Turn we to God by trial of our ways;
To heav'n our hearts, our hands, and voices raise.
We have transgress'd, rebell'd; no pardon gain;
The food of wrath; by Thee pursu'd and slain.
Thou hast with clouds Thyself inclos'd of late,
Through which no pray'rs of ours can penetrate.
With men the refuse and offscouring made,
Whom all our foes with open mouths upbraid.
Fill'd with vastation, ruins, snares, and fears,
While for my children's loss I melt in tears.
Nor shall those briny rivers cease to flow,
Till God look down with pity on our woe.
Mine eye, ah! wounds my heart, when I behold
My city's daughters to afflictions sold.
Those who thy beauty, Solyma, deface,
My soul like a retrievéd partridge chase:
Cut from the living, in a dungeon thrown,
And overwhelméd with a pile of stone.
Storms o'er my head their rolling billows tost;
Then cried I: Ah! I am for ever lost!
Thou from the dungeon, Lord, my cries didst hear;
O never from my sighs divert Thine ear!

Thou stood'st beside me in that horrid day,
And said'st: Take courage, nor thy fear obey.
My cause, Thou, Lord, hast pleaded in this strife,
And from their greedy jaws redeem'd my life.
Thou that hast seen my wrongs, restore my right;
Thou hast their vengeance seen and cursèd spite;
The malice heard which their false tongues disclose,
The thoughts and machinations of my foes.
When they sit down, and when they rise, I still
Become their music, and their laughter fill.
Rewards according to their works disburse;
Their hearts with sorrow wound, blast with Thy
    curse.
Pursue, destroy ; nor, Lord, Thy wrath restrain,
Till none beneath the arch of heav'n remain.

CHAPTER IV.

OW is our gold grown dim ! of all the most
Refin'd and pure hath now his lustre lost !
That marble, which the temple beautified,
Torn down by impious rage, and cast aside.
The wretched sons of Sion, ah ! behold,
Of late so precious, more esteem'd than gold,
How slighted ! to how low a value brought !
Like earthen vessels by the potter wrought !
The monsters of the sea, and savage beasts,
Their young ones gently foster at their breasts :
My daughters, ah ! more cruel are than these,
Or than the desert-haunting estriches.
Their children cry for bread, but none receive,
Whose thirsty tongues to their hot palates cleave.
Who fed deliciously, now sit forlorn ;
And those who scarlet wore, on dung-hills mourn.
The punishments, as did their sins, excell
That which from heav'n on wicked Sodom fell,

Devour'd with sudden flames. No creature found
To whom His wrath could add another wound.
Her Nazarites, late pure as falling snow,
More white than streams which from stretch'd
    udders flow;
Not rubies of the rock such red inspher'd,
Nor polish'd sapphires like their veins appear'd;
Their faces now more black than cinders grown,
To such as meet them in the streets unknown;
Whose wither'd skins, more dry than sapless wood,
Cleave to their fleshless bones for want of food.
O far less wretched they, whose parting breath
Breaks through their wounds, than those who
    starve to death!
For they in ling'ring torments pine away,
And find not death so cruel as delay.
Soft-hearted mothers live by horrid spoil,
And their belovéd babes in cauldrons boil.
On these with weeping eyes, and hearts that bleed,
The famish'd daughters of my people feed.
The Lord His vengeance now accomplish'd hath,
And pouréd forth the vials of His wrath;
Forsaken Sion sets on fire, whose tow'rs
And palaces the hungry flame devours.
You kings that sway the many-peopl'd earth,
All who from groaning mothers take your birth,
O would you have believ'd that thus the foe
Should have triumph'd in her sad overthrow?
Her priests' and prophets' sins, who should have
    taught
By their example, have her ruin wrought;
With human flesh her flaming altars fed,
And blood of innocents profusely shed.
Who blindly wander, so defil'd with gore,
That none would touch the garments which they
    wore.

LAMENTATIONS OF JEREMIAH. 369

Depart, they cried, depart, and touch us not,
Depart, O you whom foul pollutions spot.
Thus chid, they stray'd, and to the Gentiles fled,
Yet said, ere long we shall from hence be led.
For this, the Lord hath scatter'd in His ire,
Nor ever shall they to their homes retire:
Their unregarded priests slain by the foe,
Who would no pity to the aged show.
Yet vainly we, in these our miseries,
With expectation have consum'd our eyes,
And foster'd flatt'ring hopes; built on their word,
Who can no aid to our extremes afford.
Like cruel hunters, they our steps pursue,
While we in corners lurk from public view.
That fatal day draws near, wherein we must
Descend to death and mingle with the dust.
Not eagles fearful doves so swiftly chase,
As they with wingéd feet our footsteps trace,
Pursue o'er mountains, watch at ev'ry strait,
And to entrap us in the desert wait.
The Lord's anointed, ev'n our nostrils' breath,
They have ensnar'd, and render'd up to death.
Of whom we said: Among the heathen we,
Beneath his wings, shall live in exile free.
Daughter of Edom, thou that dwell'st in Hus,
Exalt thy joy: this cup to thee from us
Shall swiftly pass; thy brains inebriate so,
As thou thy nakedness shalt boldly show.
Yet when thy sins' deservéd punishment,
O wretched Sion's daughter, shall be spent,
Jehovah will thy banishment repeal,
Foment thy wounds, and all thy bruises heal.
Then He on Edom's issue shall impose
Our yoke, and her deformity disclose.

Chap V.

REMEMBER, Lord, th' afflictions we have borne,
See how we are to all the world a scorn!
Our lands and houses foreigners possess,
Our mothers widows, and we fatherless.
To us our wood the greedy stranger sells,
And dearly-purchas'd water from our wells.
Our necks with heavy burdens are oppress'd;
All day we toil, at night depriv'd of rest.
We, in th' Egyptian and Assyrian lands,
Are forc'd to beg our bread with stretch'd-out hands.
Our fathers, who transgress'd, in death remain,
And we the pressure of their sins sustain.
Who were our vassals, now our sovereigns are,
And none survive to comfort our despair.
With peril of our lives we seek our food,
The sword in pathless deserts thirsts for blood,
While storms of famine mutiny within,
And, like a furnace, tan the sapless skin.
In Judah's cities virgins they deflow'r,
In Sion ravish'd wives their wrongs deplore.
They crucify our princes in their rage,
Nor honour the aspéct of rev'rend age.
Our youth enforce to grind, with lashes gall,
And boys beneath their cruel burdens fall.
No judge on high tribunals now appears,
No music draws our souls into our ears;
Joy from our broken hearts exiléd flies,
Our mirth is chang'd to mourning elegies.
The crown from our eclipséd brows is torn;
By all, except Thy punishments, forlorn.
Woe to our sins! for these we waste our years
In servitude. We drown our eyes with tears

LAMENTATIONS OF JEREMIAH.

For thee, deserted Sion ! Foxes dwell
Among thy ruins. Who our woes can tell?
Yet, Lord, Thou ever liv'st: Thy throne shall last
When funeral flames the world to cinders waste.
O why hast Thou so long forgot Thine own?
Wilt Thou forsake us as if never known ?
O call us back, that we Thy Face may view,
Those happy days we once enjoy'd renew.
But Thou hast cast us off, to tread the path
Of exile ; made the object of thy wrath.

THE END OF THE LAMENTATIONS OF JEREMIAH.

A PARAPHRASE

UPON THE SONGS COLLECTED OUT OF THE OLD AND NEW TESTAMENTS.

A PARAPHRASE

UPON THE SONGS COLLECTED OUT OF THE

OLD AND NEW TESTAMENTS.

EXODUS XV.

PART I. *Tune 7.*

THE praise of our triumphant King,
And of His victory we sing,
Who in the seas with horrid force
O'erthrew the rider and his horse.
My Strength, my God, my Argument,
My father's God, hath safety sent.
To Him will I a mansion raise,
There celebrate His glorious praise.
His sword hath won eternal fame,
And Great Jehovah is His Name.
Lo! Pharaoh's chariots, his proud host,
Are in the swallowing billows lost.
God, in the fathomless profound,
Hath all his choice commanders drown'd.
Down sunk they, like a falling stone,
By raging whirlpits overthrown.

Thy pow'rful Hand these wonders wrought,
Our foes by Thee to ruin brought.
Thou, all that durst against Thee fight,
Hast crush'd by Thy prevailing might.
Thy wrath Thy foes to cinders turns,
As fire the sun-dried stubble burns.

Part II.

Blown by Thy nostrils' breath, the flood
In heaps, like solid mountains, stood.
The sea's divided heart congeal'd,
Her sandy bottom first reveal'd.
Pursue, o'ertake, th' Egyptians cried,
Let us their wealthy spoil divide;
Our sword these fugitives destroy,
And with their slaughter feast our joy.
Thou blew'st; those hills their billows spread,
In mighty seas they sunk like lead.
What god is like our God? so high!
So excellent in sanctity!
Whose glorious praise such terror breeds,
So wonderful in all Thy deeds!
Thy Hand outstretch'd, the closing womb
Of waves gave all his host one tomb.
But us, who have Thy Mercy tried,
In our redemption, Thou wilt guide:
Guide by Thy pow'r, till we possess
The mansion of Thy holiness.

Part III.

Our foes shall this with terror hear,
Sad Palestine grow pale with fear.
Those who the Edomites command,
And Moab's chiefs, shall trembling stand.

EXODUS XV.

The hearts of Canaan melt away,
Like snow before the sun's bright ray.
Horror shall seize on all; not one
But stand like statues cut in stone,
Until Thy people pass; ev'n those
Whom Thou hast ransom'd from their foes.
Thou shalt conduct and plant them where
Thy fruitful hills their shoulders rear;
By Thy election dignified,
Where Thou for ever shalt abide.
Thy reign, Eternal King, shall last
When heav'n and earth in vapours waste.
While Pharaoh's chariots and his horse
'Twixt walls of seas their way enforce,
Thy Hand reduc'd th' obedient waves,
Which clos'd them in their rolling graves;
But Israel through the bottom sand
Securely pass'd, as on dry land.

DEUTERONOMY XXXII.

Part I. *Tune 1.*

END, O you heav'ns, unto my voice an ear,
And thou, O earth, what I shall utter, hear.
My words shall fall like dew, like April showers
On tender herbs and new-disclosèd flowers,
While I the goodness of our God proclaim :
O celebrate His great and glorious Name!
Our Rock, Whose works are perfect. Justice leads,
And equal judgment walks the way He treads.

In Him unstain'd sincerity excells ;
The God of Truth, in Whom no falsehood dwells :
But you are all corrupt, perverse ; nor bear
Those marks about you which His children wear.
O fools ! depriv'd of intellectual light !
Do you your Great Preserver thus requite ?
Your Father, He who made you, did select
From all the world, and with His beauty deck't ?
Remember,—ask the ancient,—they will tell
What in old times and ages past befell,
When the Most High did distribute the earth,
With liberal hand, to all of human birth.
When yet you were not, He, according to
Your num'rous race, design'd a seat for you.

PART II.

His people are His portion : Jacob is
Th' inheritance alone reserv'd for His.
He, when he wander'd through a desert land,
And in a horrid wilderness of sand,
Conducted, taught him His high mysteries,
And kept him as the apples of His Eyes.
As the old eagle on her eyrie spreads
Her fost'ring plumes, renews their downy beds,
Feeds, trains them for the flight, subdues their
    fears,
And on her soaring wings her eaglets bears ;
So He sustain'd, so led him ; He alone :
No stranger-gods to Israel then were known.
Whom like a horse the tow'ring mountains bore,
That those rich fields might feast him with their
    store.
With honey the hard rocks supplied his want,
And pure oil drill'd from cliffs of adamant.
Him with the milk of ewes, with butter fed,
With fat of lambs, and rams in Bashan bred.

With flesh of goats, with wheat's pure kernels
fill'd,
And drank the blood which from the grape distill'd.

PART III.

But Jesurun grew fat; kick'd like a horse
Full of high feeding and untaméd force ;
Forsook his God, Who made, sustain'd, adorn'd,
And That strong Rock of his salvation scorn'd.
With barbarous gods and execrable rites,
His jealousy and wrath at once excites.
To devils they profanely sacrific'd;
Gods made with hands before their Maker priz'd ;
Gods brought from foreign nations, strange and
new ;
Gods which their ancestors nor fear'd nor knew.
Their Father, their firm Rock, remember'd not,
And Him Who had created them forgot.
This having seen with burning eyes, the Lord
His daughters and degen'rate sons abhorr'd :
Said, From these rebels I will hide My Face,
And see the end of this unfaithful race.
Since they with gods, that are but gods in name,
My Soul with so great jealousy inflame,
And through their vanities My wrath incense,
I by the like will punish their offence,
Their glory to an unknown nation grant,
And in their room a foolish people plant.

PART IV.

A fire is kindled in My wrath, which shall
Ev'n in the depth of hell devour them all ;
Polluted earth, with her productions, burn,
And airy mountains into ashes turn.

One misery another shall invite,
And all My arrows in their bosoms light.
Famine shall eat them, hot diseases burn,
And all by violent deaths to earth return.
The teeth of savage beasts their blood shall spill,
And serpents with their fatal poison kill.
The sword without, and home-bred terrors, shall
Devour their lives, their youth untimely fall.
Betrothéd virgins, such as stoop with age,
And sucking babes, shall sink beneath My rage.
Scatter I would, like chaff by tempests blown,
Nor should their memory to man be known,
If not withheld by their insulting foe,
Lest he should triumph in their overthrow,
And boasting say: This our own hands have done;
Our swords, the gods which have their battle won.

PART V.

A nation which hath no intelligence,
Uncapable of counsel, void of sense,
O! that My words could to their hearts descend,
To make them wise and think of their last end!
How would one man a thousand put to flight,
And two a myriad overthrow in fight!
But that their Strength hath sold them to their
    foes,
And left them naked to their deadly blows.
For, though our enemies should judge, their
    pow'rs
Are faint to His; their rock no rock to ours.
Their vine of Sodom, of Gomorrah's fields,
Which grapes of gall and bitter clusters yields.
Poison of dragons is their deadly wine,
To which cold asps their drowsy venom join.
Is not all this unto My sight reveal'd?
Laid up in store, and with My signet seal'd?

To Me belongs revenge and recompense,
Which I will in the time decreed dispense.
The day is near which their destruction brings,
And punishment now flies with speedy wings.

PART VI.

God will His people judge, at length relent,
And of His servants' miseries repent,
Then, when they are of all their pow'r bereft,
No strength, no hope of human succour left,
And say : Where are the gods of your defence,
Those rocks of your presuming confidence,
Whose flaming altars ye so often fed
With fat of beeves, and wine profusely shed?
Now let them from their crownéd banquets rise,
And shield you from your furious enemies.
Behold ! I am your God: I, only I,
Assisted by no foreign deity.
I kill, revive; I wound and heal; no hand
Or pow'r of mortals can My strength withstand.
I, to the heav'ns I made, My arms extend;
Pronounce, I ever was, and have no end.
Whet I My glitt'ring sword, if I advance
My Hand in judgment, woes past utterance,
And vengeance equal to their merits, shall
Upon My foes, and those who hate Me, fall.
The hungry sword shall eat their flesh like food,
My thirsty arrows shall be drunk with blood.
For captives slain, and for the blood they spilt,
I will with horror recompence their guilt.
You wiser nations with His people joy,
For He will all their enemies destroy,
His servants vindicate from their proud foe,
And to their land and them His mercy show.

JUDGES V.

PART I. *Tune 7.*

YOUR Great Preserver celebrate,
He who reveng'd our wrongs of late!
When you His sons, in Israel's aid,
Of life so brave a tender made.
You princes, with attention hear,
And you who awful sceptres bear,
While I in sacred numbers sing
The praise of our Eternal King.
When He through Seir His army led,
In Edom's fields His ensigns spread,
Earth shook, the heav'ns in drops descend,
And clouds in tears their substance spend.
Before His Face the mountains melt,
Old Sinai unknown fervour felt.
When Israel Sangar's rule obey'd,
And Jael, that virágo, sway'd;
She bold of heart, he great in war;
Yet to the fearful traveller
All ways were then unsafe, who crept
Through woods, or pass'd when others slept.
The land uncultivated lay:
When I arose, I Deborah,
A mother to my country grew,
At once their foes and fears subdue.

PART II.

When to themselves new gods they chose,
Then were their walls besieg'd by foes.
Did one of forty thousand wear
A coat of steel? or shook a spear?
You, who with such alacrity
Led to the battle, O how I

JUDGES V.

Affect your valour! with me raise
Your voices; sing Jehovah's praise.
Sing you, who on white asses ride,
And justice equally divide;
You, who those ways so fear'd of late,
Where now no thieves assassinate;
You lately from your fountains barr'd,
Where you their clatt'ring quivers heard;
There, with united joy record
The righteous judgments of the Lord.
You, who your cities repossess,
Who reap in peace, His praise profess.
Arise, O Deborah, arise,
In heav'nly hymns express thy joys.
Arise, O Barak, thou the fame
And offspring of Abinoam,
Of Israel the renownéd head,
Captivity now captive led.

PART III.

Nor shall the noble memory
Of our strong aids in silence die.
The quiver-bearing Ephraimite
March'd from his mountain to the fight.
Those who on Amalek confine;
The small remains of Benjamin;
From Machir, princes; not a few
Wise Zebulun with letters drew:
The valiant chiefs of Issachar,
With Deborah, troop'd to this war;
Who down into the valley tread
The way which noble Barak led.
But Reuben, from the rest disjoin'd
By hills and floods, was so in mind.

Did'st thou these glorious wars refuse,
To hear the bleating of the ewes?
O great in council! O how wise!
That couldst both faith and fame despise.
Gilead, of thund'ring drums afraid,
Or slothful, beyond Jordan staid.
Dan his swift-sailing ships affects,
And public liberty neglects:
While Ashur on his cliffs resides,
And fortifies against the tides.
But Zebulun and Naphthali,
Who never would from danger fly,
Were ready, for the public good,
On Tabor's top to shed their blood.

PART IV.

Then kings, kings of the Canaanites,
On Taanach plains address'd their fights,
Where swift Megiddo's waters ran;
Yet neither spoil nor trophy wan.
The heav'ns 'gainst Sisera fought; the stars
Mov'd in battalia to those wars;
By ancient Kishon swept from thence,
Whose torrent falling clouds incense.
Thou, O my joyful soul, at length
Hast trod to dirt their puissant strength.
Their wounded horse with flying haste
Fall headlong, and their riders cast.
Thus spake an angel: Cursed be
Thou Meroz, all who dwell in thee;
That basely would'st no aid afford,
In that great battle, to the Lord.
Cinœian Heber's wife, thou best
Of women, be thou ever blest;

JUDGES V.

Blest above all; let all that dwell
In tents thy act, O Jael, tell.
She brought him milk above his wish,
And butter in a princely dish.
A hammer and a nail she took,
This into Sisera's temples struck.
He fell, fell down, down to the floor;
Lay where he fell, bath'd in his gore;
Lay grovelling at her feet; and there
His wretched soul sigh'd into air.

PART V.

His mother at her window stay'd,
And thrusting out her shoulders said,
Why are his chariot's wheels so slow,
Nor yet my son in triumph show?
When her wise ladies, standing by,
(Yea she herself) made this reply,
Have not their swords now won the day?
Have they not shar'd the wealthy prey?
Now ev'ry soldier for his pains
An Hebrew dame or virgin gains;
While Sisera, choosing, lays aside
Rich robes in various colours dy'd;
Rich robes with curious needles wrought
On either side, from Phrygia brought,
The thread spun from the silk-worms' womb,
Such as a conqueror become.
Great God! so perish all Thy foes!
Love such as love Thee: O let those
Shine like the sun, when he displays
In th' orient his increasing rays.

I. SAMUEL II.

Part I.
Tune 15.

GOD hath rais'd my head on high:
O my heart, enlarge thy joy!
God hath now my tongue untied,
To retort their scorn and pride.
In Thy grace I will rejoice;
Praise Thee, while I have a voice.
Who so holy as our Lord?
Who but He to be ador'd?
Who such wonders can effect?
Who so strongly can protect?
Be no longer arrogant,
Nor in folly proudly vaunt:
God our secret thoughts displays;
All our works His balance weighs.
Giants' bows His forces break;
He with strength invests the weak.
Who were full, now serve for bread;
Those who serv'd, enfranchiséd.
Barren wombs with children flow;
Fruitful mothers childless grow.

Part II.

God frail man of life deprives;
Those who sleep in death revives:
Leads us to our silent tombs;
Brings us from those horrid rooms:
Riches sends; sends poverty;
Casteth down, and lifts on high.
He from the despiséd dust,
From the dunghill, takes the just;

To the height of honour brings,
Plants them in the thrones of kings.
God earth's mighty pillars made;
He the world upon them laid.
He His servants' feet will guide;
Wicked souls, who swell with pride,
Will in endless darkness chain,
Since all human strength is vain.
He shall grind His enemies,
Blast with lightning from the skies:
Judge the habitable earth,
All of high and humble birth:
Shall with strength His King renown,
And His Christ with glory crown.

II. SAMUEL I.

Tune 19.

THY beauty, Israel, is fled,
    Sunk to the dead.
How are the valiant fall'n! the slain
    Thy mountains stain.
O let it not in Gath be known,
Nor in the streets of Ascalon!

Lest that sad story should excite
    Their dire delight:
Lest in the torrent of our woe
    Their pleasure flow:
Lest their triumphant daughters ring
Their cymbals, and curs'd pæans sing.

You hills of Gilboa, never may
    You off'rings pay:
No morning dew, nor fruitful showers,
    Clothe you with flowers:

Saul and his arms there made a spoil,
As if untouch'd with sacred oil.

The bow of noble Jonathan
    Great battles wan;
His arrows on the mighty fed,
    With slaughter red.
Saul never rais'd his arm in vain,
His sword still glutted with the slain.

How lovely! O how pleasant! when
    They liv'd with men!
Than eagles swifter, stronger far
    Than lions are:
Whom love in life so strongly tied,
The stroke of death could not divide.

Sad Israel's daughters, weep for Saul;
    Lament his fall:
Who fed you with the earth's increase,
    And crown'd with peace:
With robes of Tyrian purple deck'd,
And gems which sparkling light reflect.

How are thy worthies by the sword
    Of war devour'd!
O Jonathan, the better part
    Of my torn heart!
The savage rocks have drunk thy blood:
My brother! O how kind! how good!

Thy love was great; O never more
    To man, man bore!
No woman, when most passionate,
    Lov'd at that rate!
How are the mighty fall'n in fight!
They and their glory set in night!

2 SAMUEL VII.

Part I. *Tune 4.*

Y Lord, my God, O who am I,
Or what is my poor family,
    That Thou should'st crown,
    With pow'r renown,
And raise my throne on high?

As this were little, in my place
Hast promis'd to confirm my race.
    Do men, O Lord,
    To men afford
Such, such transcendent grace?

Not to be hop'd for nor desir'd,
Not to be utter'd, but admir'd:
    My thoughts to me,
    Than they to Thee,
Less known when most retir'd.

These great things did'st Thou to fulfill
Thy word and never-changing will.
    Into my sight
    This knowing light
Thy wisdom's beams distill.

In goodness as in pow'r complete,
No God but Thee : O who so great?
    All this of old
    Our fathers told,
And often did repeat.

What nation breathes who can or dare
With thee, O Israel, compare?
    For whom alone
    God left His throne,
As His peculiar care.

To amplify His Name; to do
Such great, such fearful things for you;
    Such wonders wrought;
    From Egypt brought;
From men, from gods withdrew.

Establish'd by divine decree,
That Thou might be our God, and we
    For evermore
    Thy Name adore,
As consecrate to Thee.

PART II.

Now, Lord, effect what Thou hast said,
The promise to Thy servant made.
    Confirm by deed
    What to his seed
Thy word long since display'd.

Great God, O be Thou magnified,
Whose Hands the strife of war decide!
    Let David's race
    Before Thy Face
For ever fix'd abide.

Thou saidst (Who Israel dost protect)
I will My servant's house erect.
    My thoughts indu'd
    With gratitude
These pray'rs to Thee direct.

Thou, Lord, in goodness infinite!
Whose word and truth like twins unite.
    Thy promise hath
    Confirm'd my faith,
And fill'd me with delight.

Be then my house for ever bless'd,
Of Thy dear Presence still possess'd.
　　Thus hast Thou said,
　　This promise made :
O with Thy grace invest !

ISAIAH V.

Tune 8.

NOW I to My Belovéd will
　　A song of My Belovéd sing :
　　He hath a vineyard on a hill,
Which all the year enjoy'd the spring.
This He incloséd with a mound,
　　Pick'd up the stones which scatter'd lay :
With gen'rous vines plants the rich ground;
　　Digg'd, prun'd, and weeded ev'ry day.
To press the clusters made a frame,
　　Plac'd in a new-erected tow'r ;
But when th' expected vintage came,
　　For good, the grapes prov'd wild and sour.
You who on Judah's hills reside,
　　Who citizens of Salem be,
Do you the controverse decide,
　　Between My vineyard judge, and Me.
Though partial, judge.　Could I have more
　　To My ungrateful vineyard done ?
Yet such unpleasant clusters bore,
　　Unworthy of the soil or sun.
Then know : This vineyard, late My joy,
　　Manuréd with such diligence,
Wild boars and foxes shall destroy,
　　When I have trampled down her fence.
Then shall she unregarded lie,
　　Undigg'd, unprun'd, with brambles spread ;

No gentle clouds shall on her dry
    And thirsty womb their moisture shed.
That ancient house of Israel
    The Great Jehovah's vineyard is;
They who on Judah's mountains dwell,
    Those choice and pleasant plants of His:
From whom He justice did expect,
    But rapine and oppression found;
Thought they sweet concord would affect,
    When all with strife and cries abound.

ISAIAH XXVI.

PART I.

Tune 2.

OUR Sion strongly is secur'd,
    Which God Himself hath fortified;
High bulwarks rais'd on ev'ry side,
    And with immortal walls immur'd:
Her gates at their approach display,[1]
Who justice love, and truth obey.

Who fix on Him their confidence,
    He will in constant peace preserve.
O then with faith Jehovah serve,
    Your strong and ever sure Defence:
Who hurls the mighty from their thrones,
And cities turns to heaps of stones.

Their structures levels with the floor,
    Which sepulchres of dust inclose;
Trod underneath the feet of those,
    That were of late despis'd and poor.
Straight is the way the righteous tread,
By Thee at once inform'd and led.

---

[1] Display—*i. e.* open.

For we Thy judgments, Lord, expect,
And only on Thy grace rely;
To Thy great Name and memory
Th' affections of our souls erect.
My soul pursues Thee in the night,
And when the morn displays her light.

PART II.

Didst Thou Thy judgments exercise,
Then mortals should the truth discern:
And yet the wicked would not learn,
But Thy extended grace despise:
Among the just to injustice sold;
Nor will Thy Majesty behold.

Should'st Thou advance Thine arm on high,
Though wilful-blind, yet should they view
The shame and vengeance which pursue
All those who Thy dear saints envy:
Those vindicating flames, which burn
Thy foes, shall them to cinders turn.

Thou our eternal peace hast wrought,
And in our works Thy wonders shown.
Though other lords, besides our own,
Had us to their subjection brought,
Yet, through Thy only goodness, we
Remember'd both Thy Name and Thee.

Dead are they, never more to rise
From those dark caves of endless night;
Nor ever shall the cheerful light
Re-visit with their closéd eyes.
Thy vengeance hath expell'd their breath,
And clos'd their memories in death.

Part III.

Thou, Thou hast giv'n us wounds on wounds;
  In punishing Thy glory shown:
  Far from Thy cheerful presence thrown,
Ev'n to the world's extremest bounds:
  Amidst our stripes and sighings, we
  Address'd our zealous pray'rs to Thee.

As women groaning with their load,
  The time of their deliv'ry near,
  Anticipating pain with fear,
Shriek in their pangs; so we to God:
  So suffer'd, when in Thy disgrace;
  So cried out, when Thou hidd'st Thy Face.

For we, with sorrow's burthen fraught,
  Pain and anxiety of mind,
  Brought only forth an empty wind,
Nor our desir'd deliv'ry wrought.
  We neither could repulse our foes,
  Nor give a period to our woes.

The Lord thus to His people spake:
  Thy dead shall live; those who remain
  In peaceful graves shall rise again.
O you who sleep in dust, awake!
  Now sing! On you My plants I'll shed
  My dew; the graves shall cast their dead.

Go, hide thee in thy inward rooms
  A little, till My wrath pass by:
  To punish man's impiety,
The Lord from heav'n in thunder comes:
  The earth then shall your blood reveal,
  Nor longer shall the slain conceal.

ISAIAH XXXVIII.

PART I. *Tune* 19.

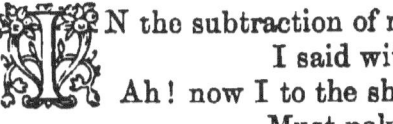N the subtraction of my years,
　　I said with tears:
Ah! now I to the shades below
　　Must naked go:
Cut off by death before my time,
And like a flow'r cropp'd in my prime.

Lord, in Thy temple I no more
　　Shall Thee adore;
No longer with mankind converse
　　In my cold hearse.
My age is past ere it be spent,
Removéd like a shepherd's tent.

My frail life, like a weaver's thread,
　　My sins have shred:
My vital pow'rs diseases waste
　　With greedy haste:
Ev'n from the evening to the day
I languish, and consume away.

And when the morning watch is past,
　　Think that my last.
Thou like a lion break'st my bones,
　　Nor hear'st my groans:
Ev'n from the dawning to the night,
Death waits to close my failing sight.

Thus swallow-like, like to a crane,
　　My woes complain:
Mourn like a turtle-dove but late
　　Robb'd of his mate.
I my dim eyes to Thee erect:
The weak O strengthen and protect!

Part II.

What praise can reach Thy clemency,
    O Thou Most High?
Thy words are ever crown'd with deeds:
    Joy grief succeeds.
My bitter pangs at length are past,
And long my peaceful days shall last.

My lively vigour dost restore,
    Increas'd with more:
My years prolong'd, now flourishing
    In their new spring:
Thou hast with joy dried up my tears,
And with my grief exil'd my fears.

Thy love hath drawn me from the pit
    Where horrors sit:
My soul-infecting sins Thou hast
    Behind Thee cast.
The grave cannot Thy praise relate,
Nor death Thy goodness celebrate.

Can They expect Thy mercy whom
    Cold earth entomb?
The living must Thy truth display,
    As I this day.
This fathers to their sons shall tell,
While souls in human bodies dwell.

The Lord as ready was to save,
    As I to crave:
I therefore to the warbling string
    His praise will sing:
And in His house, till my last day,
My grateful vows devoutly pay.

JONAH I.
Tune 8.

IN Thee my captiv'd soul did call,
  Thou, Who art present ev'rywhere,
  From the dark entrails of the whale,
Didst thy entombéd servant hear.
Thy Hand into the surges threw,
  The sea's black arms forthwith unfold,
Down to the horrid bottom drew,
  And all her waves upon me roll'd.
Then said my soul: For ever I
  Am banish'd from Thy glorious sight;
And yet Thy temple with the eye
  Of faith review'd in that blind night.
The floods my soul involv'd below,
  The swallowing deeps besieg'd me round,
And weeds, which in the bottom grow,
  My head with funeral dresses bound.
I to the roots of mountains div'd,
  Whom bars of broken rocks restrain;
Yet from that tomb of death reviv'd,
  And rais'd to see the sun again.
I, when my soul began to faint,
  My vows and pray'rs to Thee preferr'd;
The Lord my passionate complaint,
  Ev'n from His holy temple, heard.
Those who affect false vanities,
  The mercy of their God betray;
But I my thanks will sacrifice,
  And vows to my Redeemer pay.

HABAKKUK III.

Part I. *Tune* 22.

GREAT God, with terror I have heard Thy
    doom,
The fearful punishments that are to come:
Yet in the midst of those devouring years,
Then when Thy vengeance shall exceed our fears,
Thy work in us revive; confirm our faith,
And still remember mercy in Thy wrath.
God came from Theman, and the Holy One
From Paran's mountain, where His glory shone,
Which fill'd the heav'ns themselves with brighter
    rays,
And all the earth replenish'd with His praise.
His brightness as the sun's; His fingers streams
Of light project; His pow'r hid in those beams.
Devouring pestilence before Him flew,
And wasting flames His dreadful steps pursue.
Then fix'd His feet, and measur'd with His eyes
The earth's extent: pale fears her sons surprise:
The ancient mountains shrunk; eternal hills
Stoop'd to their bases; all amazement fills.
His glory and His terror He displays,
In His unknown and everlasting ways.
I saw th' afflicted tents of Cushan quake,
And Midian's curtains in that tempest shake.

Part II.

When Thou, O Lord, the rivers didst divide,
And on the chariots of salvation ride,
Through the congested billows of the seas,
Was it because Thou wast displeas'd with these?
According to Thy oath Thou drew'st Thy sword;
Thy oath sworn to our tribes, Thy constant word.

HABAKKUK III.

From cloven rocks new torrents took their flight,
And airy mountains trembled at Thy sight:
The over-flowing streams enforce their ways,
The deeps to Thee their hands and voices raise;
The sun and moon, obedient to command,
Till then in restless motion, made a stand.
Thy darts and flaming arrows, swift as sight,
Confound Thy foes, but give Thy people light.
He, in His fury, marchéd through the land,
And crush'd the heathen with a vengeful Hand.
The anointed with Thy sword their leaders slew;
The joints disclos'd where heads of princes grew.
With Thy transfixing spear their subjects strake;
Who like a black and dreadful tempest brake
Upon our front, with purpose to devour,
And triumph over our despiséd pow'r.
He through the roaring floods His people guides,
Through yielding seas on fiery horses rides.

Part III.

When I Thy threat'nings heard, my entrails shook,
And my unnervéd knees each other strook.
My lips with panting swell, my cheeks grow wan,
Through all my bones a swift consumption ran.
O where may I repose in that sad day,
When arméd troops upon my country prey!
Although the fig-tree shall no blossoms bear,
Nor vines with their pure blood the pensive cheer;
Although the olive no requital yield,
Nor corn apparel the deserted field;
Though then our flocks be ravish'd from the fold,
And though our stalls no well-fed oxen hold;
Yet will not I despair, but cheerfully
Expect, and in Thy known salvation joy:
For Thou my strength and my protection art.
My feet, more nimble than the flying hart,
Ascend the hills; where I, with holy fire,
Will sing Thy praises to my solemn lyre.

A PARAPHRASE UPON

LUKE I.
Tune 7.

MY ravish'd soul extols His Name
Who rules the world's admiréd frame :
My spirit, with exalted voice,
In God my Saviour shall rejoice :
Who hath His glorious beams display'd
Upon a poor and humble maid.
Me all succeeding ages shall
The Blessed Virgin-Mother call.
The Great great things for me hath wrought ;
His sanctity past human thought.
His mercy still reflects on those
Who in His truth their trust repose.
He with His arm hath wonders shown,
The proud in their own pride o'erthrown,
The mighty from their thrones dejects,
The lowly from the dust erects.
The hungry are His welcome guests,
The rich excluded from His feasts.
He, mindful of His promise, hath
Maintain'd and crownéd Israel's faith,
To Abraham promis'd, and decreed
For ever to his holy seed.

LUKE I.
Tune 20.

PRAISE the Lord, His wonders tell,
Whose mercy shines in Israel,
At length redeem'd from sin and hell.

The Crown of our salvatíon,
Deriv'd from David's royal throne,
He now hath to His people shown.

This to His prophets did unfold,
By all successively foretold,
Until the infant world grew old.

That He our wrongs would vindicate,
Save from our foes' inveterate hate,
And raise our long depress'd estate.

To ratify His ancient deed,
His promis'd grace, by oath decreed,
To Abraham and his faithful seed.

That we might our Preserver praise,
Walk purely in His perfect ways,
And fearless serve Him all our days.

His path Thou shalt prepare, sweet Child,
And run before the Undefil'd,
The Prophet of th' Almighty styl'd.

Our knowledge to inform, from whence
Salvation springs : from penitence,
And pardon of each foul offence.

Through mercy, O how infinite!
Of our Great God, Who clears our sight,
And from the orient sheds His light.

A leading Star t' enlighten those
Whom night and shades of death inclose,
Which that high track to glory shows.

LUKE II.

Tune 18.

THOU, Who art inthron'd on high,
In peace now let Thy servant die,
    Whose hope on Thee relies:
For Thou, Whose words and deeds are one,
At length hast Thy salvation shown
    To these my ravish'd eyes.

By Thee, before Thy Hands display'd
The heavens, and earth's foundation laid,
    Unto the world decreed
A Lamp to give the Gentiles light;
A Glory, O how infinite!
    To Israel's faithful seed.

FINIS.

GLORIA DEO IN EXCELSIS.

DEO OPT. MAX.

 THOU Who all things hast of nothing made,
Whose Hand the radiant firmament display'd,
With such an undiscernéd swiftness hurl'd
About the stedfast centre of the world;
Against whose rapid course the restless sun,
And wand'ring flames, in varied motions run,
Which heat, light, life infuse; time, night, and day
Distinguish; in our human bodies sway:
That hung'st the solid earth in fleeting air,
Vein'd with clear springs, which ambient seas repair.
In clouds the mountains wrap their hoary heads;
Luxurious valleys cloth'd with flow'ry meads:
Her trees yield fruit and shade; with liberal breasts
All creatures she (their common mother) feasts.
Then man Thy image mad'st; in dignity
In knowledge, and in beauty, like to Thee:
Plac'd in a heav'n on earth: without his toil
The ever-flourishing and fruitful soil

Unpurchas'd food produc'd : all creatures were
His subjects, serving more for love than fear.
He knew no Lord but Thee. But when he fell
From his obedience, all at once rebell,
And in his ruin exercise their might:
Concurring elements against him fight:
Troops of unknown diseases, sorrow, age,
And death, assail him with successive rage.
Hell let forth all her furies : none so great
As man to man. Ambition, pride, deceit,
Wrong arm'd with pow'r, lust, rapine, slaughter
    reign'd ;
And flatter'd vice the name of virtue gain'd.
Then hills beneath the swelling waters stood,
And all the globe of earth was but one flood :
Yet could not cleanse their guilt: the following
    race
Worse than their fathers, and their sons more
    base.
Their God-like beauty lost; sin's wretched thrall;
No spark of their Divine Original
Left unextinguish'd ; all envelopéd
With darkness; in their bold transgressions
    dead.
When Thou didst from the East a Light display,
Which render'd to the world a clearer day :
Whose precepts from hell's jaws our steps with-
    draw,
And Whose Example was a living Law :
Who purg'd us with His Blood ; the way pre-
    par'd
To Heav'n, and those long-chain'd-up doors
    unbarr'd.

How infinite Thy mercy! which exceeds
The world Thou mad'st, as well as our misdeeds!
Which greater rev'rence than Thy justice wins,
And still augments Thy honour by our sins.
O who hath tasted of Thy clemency
In greater measure or more oft than I!
My grateful verse Thy goodness shall display,
O Thou, Who went'st along in all my way,
To where the morning with perfuméd wings
From the high mountains of Panchæa springs;
To that new-found-out world, where sober night
Takes from the antipodes her silent flight;
To those dark seas, where horrid winter reigns,
And binds the stubborn floods in icy chains;
To Lybian wastes, whose thirst no show'rs assuage,
And where swoll'n Nilus cools the lions' rage.
Thy wonders in the deep have I beheld,
Yet all by those on Judah's hills excell'd:
There where the Virgin's Son His doctrine taught,
His miracles, and our redemption wrought:
Where I, by Thee inspir'd, His praises sung,
And on His Sepulchre my off'ring hung.
Which way soe'er I turn my face or feet,
I see Thy glory, and Thy mercy meet.
Met on the Thracian shores, when in the strife
Of frantic Simoans Thou preserv'dst my life.
So when Arabian thieves belay'd us round,
And when, by all abandon'd, Thee I found.
That false Sidonian wolf, whose craft put on
A sheep-soft fleece, and me Bellerophon

To ruin by his cruel letter sent,
Thou didst by Thy protecting Hand prevent.
Thou sav'dst me from the bloody massacres
Of faithless Indians; from their treach'rous wars;
From raging fevers; from the sultry breath
Of tainted air, which cloy'd the joys of death.
Preserv'd from swallowing seas, when tow'ring waves
Mix'd with the clouds, and open'd their deep graves.
From barbarous pirates ransom'd: by those taught,
Successfully with Salian Moors we fought.
Then brought'st me home in safety, that this earth
Might bury me, which fed me from my birth:
Blest with a healthful age, a quiet mind,
Content with little, to this work design'd;
Which I, at length, have finish'd by Thy aid,
And now my vows have at Thy altar paid.

JAM TETIGI PORTUM,—VALETE.

FINIS.

CHRIST'S PASSION.

A TRAGEDY;

WITH ANNOTATIONS.

BY

GEORGE SANDYS.

TO THE KING'S MOST EXCELLENT MAJESTY.

SIR,

AM bold to present you with this piece of THE PASSION, the original designed by the curious pencil of *Grotius;* whose former afflictions seem to have taught him pliable passions and art to rule the affections of others, clothing the saddest of subjects in the suitable attire of tragedy; not without the example of two ancient fathers of the Primitive Church, *Apollinarius* and *Nazianzen.* This is of both the Testaments a pathetical abstract. Those formidable wonders, effected by God in His own Commonwealth; those stupendous miracles, for truth a pattern to all history, for strangeness to all fables; here meet together to attend on CHRIST'S PASSION. The effects of His power here sweetly end in those of His mercy; and That terrible Lord of Hosts is now This meek God of Peace, reconciling all to one another, and mankind to Himself. SIR, in this change of language I am no punctual interpreter: a way as servile as ungraceful. There is a fault, which painters call, too much to the life. *Quintilian* censures one, that he more affected similitude than beauty, who would have shown

greater skill if less of resemblance: the same in poetry is condemned by *Horace*, of that art the great law-giver. Thus, in the shadow of your absence, dismissed from arms by an act of time, have I, in what I was able, continued to serve you.

The humblest of your Majesty's Servants,
GEORGE SANDYS.

THE Tragedy of CHRIST's PASSION was first written in Greek by *Apollinarius* of *Laodicea*, Bishop of *Hierapolis*, and after him by *Gregory Nazianzen;* though this, now extant in his works, is by some ascribed to the former, by others accounted supposititious, as not agreeing with his strain in the rest of his poems, which might alter in that particular upon his imitation of *Euripides*. But *Hugo Grotius* of late hath transcended all on this argument: whose steps afar off I follow.

TO THE AUTHOR.

UR age's wonder; by thy birth the fame
Of *Belgia*, by thy banishment the shame;
Who to more knowledge younger didst
 arrive
Than forward *Glaucias*, yet art still alive.
Whose masters oft (for suddenly you grew
To equal and pass those, and need no new)
To see how soon how far thy wit could reach,
Sat down to wonder when they came to teach.
Oft then would *Scaliger* contented be
To leave to mend all times to polish thee,
And of that pain's effect did highlier boast
Than had he gain'd all that his[1] fathers lost.
When thy *Capella* read (which till thy hand
Had clear'd, few grave and learn'd did understand,
Though well thou might'st at such a tender age
Have made ten lessons of the plainest page)
That king of critics stood amaz'd to see
A work so like his own set forth by thee:
Nor with less wonder on that work did look
Than if the bridegroom[2] had begot the book.
To whom thy age and act seem'd to unite
At once the youth of Phœbus and the light:

---

[1] Verona.   [2] Mercury in it marries Philosophy.

TO THE AUTHOR.

Thence lov'd thee with a never-dying flame,
As the adopted heir to all his fame;
For which care, wonder, love, thy riper days
Paid him with just and with eternal praise.
Who gain'd more honour from one verse of thine,
Than all the *Canés* of his princely line:
In that he joy'd, and that oppos'd to all,
To *Titius*' spite, to hungry *Schoppius*' gall,
To what (with cause disguis'd)[1] *Bonarccius* writes,
To *Delrio's* rage, and all his *Loyolites*
But though to thee each tongue, each art be known,
As all thy time that had employ'd alone;
Though truth do naked to thy sight appear,
And scarce can we doubt more than thou canst
    clear;
Though thou at once dost different glories join,
A lofty poet and a deep divine;
Canst in the purest phrase clothe solid sense,
Scevola's law in *Tully's* eloquence;
Though thy employments have excell'd thy pen,
Show'd thee much skill'd in books, but more in
    men,
And prov'd thou canst, at the same easy rate,
Correct an author and uphold a state;
Though this rare praise do a full truth appear
To *Spain* and *Germany*, who more do fear
(Since thou thy aid did'st to that state afford)
The *Swedish* councils than the *Swedish* sword:
All this yet of thy worth makes but a part,
And we admire thy head less than thy heart;
Which (when in want) yet was too brave to close
(Though woo'd) with thy ungrateful country's foes;
When their chief ministers strove to entice
And would have bought thee at whatever price.

---

[1] Scribanius, justly ashamed of his right name.

TO THE AUTHOR.

Since all our praise and wonder is too small
For each of these, what shall we give for all?
All that we can, we do: a pen divine,
And differing only in the tongue from thine,
Doth thy choice labours with success rehearse,
And to another world transplants thy verse,
At the same height to which before they rose,
When they forc'd wonder from unwilling foes.
Now *Thames* with *Ganges* may thy labours praise,
Which there[1] breed faith, and here devotion raise.
Though your acquaintance all of worth pursue,
And count it honour to be known to you,
I dare affirm your catalogue does grace
No one who better doth deserve a place;
None hath a larger heart, a fuller head,
For he hath seen as much as you have read.
The nearer countries pass'd, his steps have press'd
The new-found world, and trod the sacred East,
Where, his brows' due, the lofty palms do rise,
Where the proud Pyramids invade the skies;
And, as all think who his rare friendship own,
Deserves no less a journey to be known.
Ulysses, if we trust the *Grecian* song,
Travell'd not far, but was a prisoner long,
To that by tempest forc'd; nor did his voice
Relate his fate: his travels were his choice,
And all those numerous realms, return'd again,
Anew he travell'd over with his pen,
And, *Homer* to himself, doth entertain
With truths more useful than his muse could fain.
Next *Ovid's Transformations* he translates
With so rare art, that those which he relates
Yield to this transmutation, and the change

---

[1] His "*De Veritate Religionis Christianæ*," intended to convert the Indians.

Of men to birds and trees appears not strange.
Next the Poetic parts of Scripture on
His loom he weaves, and *Job* and *Solomon*
His pen restores with all that heav'nly quire,
And shakes the dust from *David's* solemn lyre:
For which from all with just consent he wan
The title of the *English Buchanan*.

  Now to you both, great pair, indebted thus,
And like to be, be pleas'd to succour us
With some instructions, that it may be said,
Though nothing cross'd, we would that all were
    paid.
Let us, at least, be honest bankrouts thought,
For now we are so far from off'ring aught
Which from our mighty debt some part might take,
Alas! we cannot tell what wish to make:
For though you boast not of the wealth of *Ind*,
And though no diadems your temples bind,
No pow'r or riches equals your renown,
And they which wear such wreaths need not a
    crown.
Souls which your high and sacred raptures know,
Nor by sin humbled to our thoughts below,
Who, whilst of Heav'n the glories they recite,
Find it within, and feel the joys they write,
Above the reach or stroke of fortune live,
Not valuing what she can inflict or give;
For low desires depress the loftiest state,
But who looks down on vice looks down on fate.

FALKLAND.

THE PERSONS.

JESUS.
CHORUS OF JEWISH WOMEN.
PETER.
PONTIUS PILATE.
CAIAPHAS.
JUDAS.
THE JEWS.
FIRST NUNCIUS.
SECOND NUNCIUS.
CHORUS OF ROMAN SOLDIERS.
JOSEPH OF ARIMATHEA.
NICODEMUS.
JOHN.
MARY, THE MOTHER OF JESUS.

CHRIST'S PASSION.

THE FIRST ACT.

JESUS.

 THOU Who govern'st what Thou didst
create
With equal sway, Great Arbiter of fate,
The world's Almighty Father; I, Thy
  Son,
Though born in time, before his course begun;
Thus far my deeds have answer'd Thy com-
  mands: 5
If more remain, My zeal preparéd stands
To execute Thy charge; all that I fear,
All that I hate, I shall with patience bear;
No misery refuse, no toil, nor shame.
I know for this into the world I came. 10
And yet how long shall these extremes endure?
What day or night have known My life secure?
My burthen, by enduring, heavier grows,
And present ills a way to worse disclose.
My Kingdom, Heav'n, I left, to visit earth, 15
And suffer'd banishment before My birth.
An unknown Infant, in a stable born,
Lodg'd in a manger; little, poor, forlorn,
And miserable: though so vile a thing,
Yet worthy of the envy of a king. 20

E E

Two years scarce yet complete, too old was thought
By Herod's fears: while I alone was sought,
The bloody sword Ephratian dames deprives
Of their dear babes; through wounds they exhal'd
  their lives.
Secur'd by flying to a foreign clime, 25
The tyrant thro' his error lost his crime.
A thousand miracles have made Me known
Through all the world, and My extraction shown.
Envy against Me raves; yet virtue hath
More storms of mischief rais'd than Herod's wrath.
Is it decreed by Thy unchanging Will,
I should be acknowledg'd and rejected still?
Th' inspiréd Magi from the Orient came,
Preferr'd My star before their Mithra's flame,
And at My infant feet devoutly fell: 35
But Abraham's seed, the House of Israel,
To Thee sequester'd from eternity,
Degenerate and ingrate! their God deny.
Behold the contumacious Pharisees,
Arm'd with dissembl'd zeal, against Me rise: 40
The bloody priests to their stern party draw
The doctors of their unobservéd law:
And impious Sadducees, to perpetrate
My intended overthrow incense the state.
What rests to quicken faith? Ev'n at My nod
Nature submits, acknowledging her God.
The Galilean youth drink the pure blood
Of generous grapes, drawn from the neighbour
  flood.
I others' famine cur'd, subdu'd My own,
Life-strengthening food for forty days unknown.
'Twixt the dispensers' hands th' admiréd bread 51
Increas'd, great multitudes of people fed,
Yet more than all remain'd. The winds assuage
Their storms; and threat'ning billows calm their
  rage.

A TRAGEDY. 419

The harden'd waves unsinking feet endure: 55
And pale diseases, which despise their cure,
My Voice subdues. Long darkness chas'd away,
To Me the blind by birth now owes his day.
He hears who never yet was heard; now speaks,
And in My praises first his silence breaks. 60
Those damnéd spirits of infernal night,
Rebels to God, and to the sons of light
Inveterate foes, My Voice but heard, forsake
The long-possess'd, and struck with terror quake.
Nor was't enough for Christ, such wonders done,
To profit those alone who see the sun: 66
To vanquish Death My pow'rful Hand invades
His silent regions and inferior shades.
The stars, the earth, the seas, My triumphs know :
What rests to conquer but the deeps below ? 70
Thro' op'ning sepulchres, night's gloomy caves,
The violated privilege of graves,
I sent My dread commands : a heat new-born
Re-animates the dead, from funerals torn ;
And death's numb cold expuls'd, inforc'd a way
For souls departed to review the day.
The ashes from their ransack'd tombs receive
A second life, and by My bounty breathe.
But Death, his late free empire thus restrain'd,
Not uséd to restore his spoils, complain'd 80
That I should thus unweave the web of fate,
Decrease his subjects, and subvert his state :
I, for so many ransoméd from death,
Must to his anger sacrifice My breath.
And now that horrid hour is almost come, 85
When sinful mortals shall their Maker doom :
When I, the world's Great Lord, Who life on all
Mankind bestow'd, must by their fury fall.
That tragic time to My last period hastes ;
And night, who now on all her shadows casts,
While with the motion of the heav'ns she flies,

CHRIST'S PASSION.

This short delay of My sad life envies.
Fate, be less stern in thy intended course;
Nor drag Him Who will follow without force.
After so many miseries endur'd; 95
Cold, heat, thirst, famine, eyes to tears inur'd;
The end, yet worst of ills, draws near: their breath,
For whom I suffer, must procure My death.
The Innocent, made guilty by the foul
Defects of others, must His weary soul 100
Sigh into air; and, though of heav'nly birth,
With His chaste Blood distain th' ungrateful earth.
They traffic for My soul: My death, long sought,
Is by the mitred merchants' faction bought;
And treason finds reward. My travails draw 105
Near their last end. These practices I saw.
See what this night's confederate shadows hide:
My mind before My body crucified.
Horror shakes all My pow'rs: My entrails beat,
And all My body flows with purple sweat. 110
O whither is My ancient courage fled,
And God-like strength, by anguish captive led?
O death, how far more cruel in thy kind,
Th' anxiety and torment of the mind!
Then must I be of all at once bereft? 115
Or is there any hope of safety left?
O might I to My Heav'nly Father pray,
So supple to My tears, to take away
Part of these ills! But His eternal doom
Forbids, and order'd course of things to come. 120
His purpose, fix'd when yet the world was young,
And oracles, so oft by prophets sung,
Now rushing on their destinated end,
No orisons nor sacrifice can bend.
Why stay I with triumphant feet to tread 125
Upon th' infernal Serpent's poisonous head,
And break th' old Dragon's jaws? The sin of our

First parents must be cleansèd with a show'r
Of blood, rain'd from My wounds : My death ap-
    pease,
And cure the venom of that dire disease.   130
All you who live, rejoice : all you who die,
You sacred ashes of the just which lie
In peaceful urns, rejoice in this My fall :
I for the living liv'd, but die for all.
My suff"rings are not lost. To earth I owe 135
These promis'd ills : bonds, whips, and thorns to
    grow
About Our bleeding brows ; the Cross, the scorn
Of a proud people, to destruction borne.
O let My Father's wrath through singèd air
On Me in thunder dart, so Mine it spare.   140
Lest the world should, I perish ; and must bear
The punishments of all that ever were.
You who inhabit where the sun displays
His early light, or near his setting rays ;
Who suffer by his perpendicular   145
Aspéct, or freeze beneath the northern star ;
Affect this ready sacrifice, Who am
A Greater Off"ring than the Paschal Lamb.
My Precious Blood alone the virtue hath
To purge your sins, and quench 'My Father's
    wrath.   150
Now the full moon succeeds that vernal light
Which equally divides the day and night,
Sacred to feasts. The next sun shall survey
One brighter than himself, and lose his day.
False traitor, through thy guilt so tim'rous grown,
Although thou lead'st an army against One,
Shrouded in night, I am not taken by   156
Thy guile, but know thy fraud, and haste to die.
But you, My chosen friends, who yet preserve
Your faith entire, nor from your duty swerve,

Your festival, our washings past, rehearse
Your Maker's excellence in sacred verse;
While I to those frequented shades repair
Where the trees answer to the sighing air.
Learn, as we walk along, unto what place   165
I shortly shall return; what Heav'nly Grace
Is to descend upon you from above;
What are the laws of charity and love.
While My last pray'rs solicit Heav'n, to sleep
Give no access: this night My vigil keep.   170

CHORUS OF JEWISH WOMEN.

THE rapid motion of the spheres
Old Night from our horizon bears;
And now declining shades give way
To the return of cheerful day.
But Phosphorus, who leads the stars,   175
And day's illustrious path prepares,
Who last of all the hosts retires,
Not yet withdraws those radiant fires:
Nor have our trumpets summonéd
The morning from her dewy bed;   180
As yet her roses are unblown,
Nor by her purple mantle known.
All night we in the temple keep,
Not yielding to the charms of sleep,
That so we might with zealous pray'r   185
Our thoughts and cleanséd hearts prepare
To celebrate th' ensuing light,
When Phœbe shall her horns unite.
This annual feast to memory
Is sacred; nor with us must die: 190
Thus by that dreadful Exul taught,
When God His plagues on Egypt brought.

Those cities these our rites bereave
Of citizens, and widows leave,
Where Jordan from two bubbling heads   195
His oft-returning waters leads,
Till they their narrow bounds forsake,
And grow a sea-resembling lake.
Those woods of palm, producing dates ;
Of fragrant balsamum, which hates   200
The touch of steel ; where once the sound
Of trumpets levell'd with the ground
Unbatter'd walls ; that mount which shrouds
His airy head in hanging clouds,
Where death clos'd our lost Prophet's eyes ;   205
Admire to see their colonies
Ascend the hills of Solyma
In celebration of this day.
Cephæans, whose strong walls withstood
The ruins of the general Flood,   210
To solemnize this day, forsake
Ador'd Dercetis, and her lake.
Hither the Palestines, from strong
Azotus, both the Jamnes, throng.
Not Lydda could her own restrain ;   215
Nor Caparorsa's walls contain
Her Edomites ; Damascus could
Not hers, though she ten nations rul'd ;
Nor yet Sebaste, long the nurse
Of impious sons, sprung from our source.   220
Phœnicians, who did first produce
To mortals letters, with their use,
Where Tyrus, full of luxury,
With mother Sidon, front the sky,
Hither with hasty zeal repair :   225
Among the Syrians, those who dare
Feed on forbidden fish, nor more
The deity of a dove adore.

From Belus, whose slow waters pass
On glitt'ring sands, which turn to glass :   230
From Arnon's banks, those borderers,
The subject of our ancient wars,
Who[1] sulphurous bitumen take
From salt Asphaltis' deadly lake.
No tempest on that sea prevails;   235
No ship upon her bosom sails;
Unmov'd with oars; what over flies,
Struck by her breath, falls down and dies :
Hates all that lives; in her profound
None are receiv'd, but float undrown'd :   240
No seas, by slimy shores embrac'd,
So pestilent a vapour cast:
This blasts the corn before it bears,
And poisons the declining ears :
Sad autumn's fruits to cinders turn,   245
And all the fields in ashes mourn :
Lest time should waste the mem'ry
Of those revengeful flames, the sky
On earth in melting sulphur shower'd,
Which that accursèd race devour'd ;   250
When she, who did commiserate
With impious grief her city's fate,
Grew, in the moment of her fault,
A statue of congealéd salt.
Hither devout Esseans fly,   255
Who without issue multiply,
And virtue only propagate,
All sensual loves, all lucre hate,
And equal poverty embrace :
Thrice happy, of a noble race,   260
Who slight your own particular,
Transported with a public care.

---

[1] The old editions read: *Whose* sulphurous, &c.

A TRAGEDY.

He flies a pitch above our woes,
Or crimes, who gladly undergoes
Their toil and want; nor would possess 265
What others miscall happiness.
What numbers from the sun's uprise,
From where he leaves the morning skies,
Of our dispersed Abrahamites,
This vesper to their homes invites! 270
Yet we, in yearly triumph, still
A lamb for our deliv'rance kill.
Since liberty our confines fled,
Giv'n with the first unleaven'd bread,
She never would return; though bought 275
With wounds, and in destruction sought.
Some stray to Lybia's scorchéd sands,
Where hornéd Hammon's temple stands:
To Nilus some, where Philip's son,
Who all the rifled Orient won, 280
Built his proud city: others gone
To their old prison, Babylon:
A part to freezing Taurus fled,
And Tiber, now the ocean's head.
Our ruins all the world have fill'd: 285
But you, by use in suff'rings skill'd,
Forgetting in remoter climes
Our vanish'd glory; nor those times,
Those happy times, compare with these;
Your burdens may support with ease. 290
More justly we of Fate complain,
Who servitude at home sustain:
We, to perpetual woes design'd,
In our own country, Egypt find.

ANNOTATIONS ON THE FIRST ACT.

ERSE 23. *Ephratian Dames.*] Of Ephrata, the same with Bethlehem.

Ver. 33. *Magi.*] Tradition will have them three, of several nations, and honour them with crowns. But the word delivers them for Persians, for so they called their philosophers, such as were skilful in the celestial motions, from whence they drew their predictions; and with whom their princes consulted in all matters of moment. Some write that they were of the posterity of Balaam, by his prophecies informed of the birth of Christ, and apparition of that narrative star; but more consonant to the truth, that they received it from Divine inspiration.

Ver. 34. *My star.*] None of those which adorn the firmament; nor comet, proceeding from condensed vapours inflamed in the air; but above nature, and merely miraculous; which, as they write, not only illuminated the eye, but the understanding; excited thereby to that heavenly inquisition. Some will have it an angel in that form, the excellency whereof is thus described by Prudentius :—

"This, which in beams and beauty far
Excell'd the sun's flame-bearing car,
Show'd God's descent from heaven to earth,
Accepting of a human birth.
No servant to the humourous night,
Nor following Phœbe's changing light;
But didst thy single lamp display,
To guide the motion of the day."
Hym. Epiphaniæ.

It is probable that this star continued not above thirteen days, if we may believe that tradition, how the Magi were so long in travelling from their country unto Bethlehem.

Ver. 34. *Mithra's flame.*] Mithra: the same with the sun, adored by the Persians. His image had the countenance of a lion, with a tiara on his head, depressing an ox by the horns. Of this, Statius :—

" Come, O remember thy own temple; prove
Propitious still, and Juno's city love :
Whether we should thee rosy Titan call ;
Osiris, Lord of Ceres' festival;
Or Mithra shrined in Persian rocks, a bull,
Subduing by the horror of his skull."
Thebaid, l. 1.

And in a cave his rites were solemnized; from whence they drew an ox by the horns, which, after the singing of certain pæans, was sacrificed to the sun. Zoroaster placeth him between Oremazes and Arimanius, the good and bad dæmon, from which he took that denomination.

Ver. 39. *Pharisees.*] A precise sect among the Jews, separating themselves from others in habit, manners, and conversation, from whence they had their name, as their original from Antigonus Sochæus, who was contemporary with Alexander the Great. Men full of appearing sanctity, observant to traditions, and skilful expositors of the Mosaical Law, wearing the precepts thereof in phylacters (narrow scrolls of parchment) bound about their brows and above their left elbows; passing through the streets with a slow motion, their eyes fixed on the ground, as if ever in divine contemplations, and winking at the approach of women, by means whereof they not seldom met with churlish encounters. Superstitious in their often washing, keeping their bodies cleaner than their souls. They held that all was governed by God and fate, yet that man had the power in himself to do good or evil; that his soul was immortal; that after the death of the body, if good, it returned into another more excellent; but if evil, condemned to perpetual torments.

Ver. 43. *Sadducees.*] These derived the sect and name from Sadoc, the scholar of Antigonus Sochæus, as he his heresy, by misinterpreting the words of his master, that we should not serve God as servants, in hope of reward; concluding thereupon that in another world there was no reward for piety, and consequently no resurrection; holding the soul to be annihilated after the death of the body, herein agreeing with the Stoics:—

"As smoke from trembling flames ascends, and there,
Lost in its liberty, resolves to air;
As empty clouds, which furious tempests chase,
Consume and vanish in their airy race;
So our commanding souls fleet with our breath:
After death nothing rests; and nothing death,
But of swift life the goal. Ambition lay
Thy hopes aside, nor care our peace betray.
Inquir'st thou to what place thou shalt return
When dead? To that where lie the yet unborn."
Seneca in Troad.

They held that there were neither spirits nor angels, rejected all traditions, and only allowed of the five books of Moses; that there was no such thing as fate; that no evil proceeded from God, and that virtue and vice were in our own arbitrements. The Pharisees were sociable among themselves, but the Sadducees ever at discord, and as uncivil to their own sect as to strangers. This heresy infected not a few of the high priests; for Hircanus, with his two sons Aristobulus and Alexander, were Sadducees; so was Ananus the younger.

Ver. 151. *Now the full moon.*] In the first full moon after the sun's ascending into the equinoctial they celebrated the annual Passover according to the positive law of Moses, eating the lamb in the evening at their private houses, and lying about the table on beds, as the Romans upon their triclinium, never fewer than ten together—if they wanted of their own family, they supplied themselves with their neighbours'—nor above the number of twenty. This feast was only to be kept at Jerusalem; but those that came short of the day by reason of the distance, or were defiled with the dead, had a second passover in the month following assigned.

Ver. 161. *Our washings past.*] It was the custom as well of all the Eastern nations as of the Jews to wash the feet of their guests, though performed by inferior servants, but here by Christ Himself, to give an example of humility. They had vessels standing by ready filled with water for that purpose. This, at this feast, was observed between the first and second lying down, by way of purification.

Ver. 175. *Phosphorus.*] The same with Lucifer, which is a bringer in of light, and therefore the harbinger of the day, said to conduct and withdraw the stars in that it is the first and last that shineth. This is the beautiful planet of Venus, which, when it riseth before the sun, is the Morning star, and setting after it, the Evening.

"Now sea-bath'd Hesperus, who brings
Night on, and first displays his wings;
Now radiant Lucifer, who day
Exalting, chaseth night away."

In regard that her course is sometimes swifter than the sun, and sometimes slower, yet never far off, and fulfilling the same period.

Ver. 193. *Those cities, &c.*] The cities which lie at the foot of Libanus, on the north of Galilee, whereof Cesarea Philippi, the seat of the Tetrarch, was the principal; where Jordan not far above descends from Jor and Dan, two neighbouring fountains.

Ver. 198. *A sea-resembling lake.*] The Lake of Gennesareth, called also the Sea of Galilee, and of Tiberias, taking this name from that city there built by Antipas in honour of Tiberius. It extendeth forty furlongs in breadth, and in length an hundred; the shore once enriched with the cities of Capharnaum, Tiberias, Bethsaida, Bethsan, Gadra, Taricha, and Chorosaim.

Ver. 199. *Those woods of palms.*] In the plains adjoining to Jericho, from their abundance called the City of Palms.

Ver. 200. *Of fragrant balsamum, which, &c.*] As in Engaddi, so balsamum grew plentifully about Jericho. A plant only proper to that country, and from thence transported into Egypt by Antonius, to gratify Cleopatra. It dies if it be touched with iron, and therefore they lanch the rind with sharp stones, or knives of bone, from whence that precious liquor distilleth.

Ver. 203. *That mount.*] Phasga, from whence Moses saw all the Land of Promise from Dan to Bersheba, and there died; buried in an unknown sepulchre by an angel, lest that should have drawn the Israelites to idolatry. Saint Hierome writes how the devil, endeavouring to reveal the place, was resisted by Michael the Archangel.

Ver. 209. *Cepheans, whose strong walls, &c.*] Cepheus, the son of Phœnix, reigned in Joppa, a city built by Japhet before the Flood, and rather covered than demolished by that deluge. The inhabitants, with their territories, took the name of their king, who worshipped Dercetis, the goddess of the Ascalonites, their neighbours. She, as they fable, inflamed with the love of a beautiful youth who sacrificed unto her, having by him a daughter (who after, in that nourished by doves, was called Semiramis), ashamed of her incontinency, put away the youth, exposed the child to the mercy of the deserts, and, distracted with sorrow, threw herself into a lake near Ascalon, and there was changed into a fish. Of which Ovid :—

"To insist upon
The sad Dercetis of great Babylon;
Who, as the Palestines believe, did take
A scaly form, inhabiting a lake."

To whom a magnificent temple was erected, with her image in the likeness of a fish from the navel downwards. This was that Dagon, the idol of the Ascalonites, according to St. Hierome (by interpretation the Fish of Sorrow), which fell before the Ark of God when it was brought into her temple.

Ver. 214. *Azotus, both the Jamnes.*] Maritime towns belonging to the Philistines; the latter so called of the flourishing soil.

Ver. 215. *Lydda.*] A city seated in the valley above, and a little to the north of Joppa; called after the city of Jupiter, famous for the allegorical combat of St. George, and his martyrdom.

Ver. 216. *Caparorsa.*] A city of Judæa, according to Ptolemy; rather of Idumea, as here intimated by our author.

Ver. 217. *Damascus.*] The regal city of Syria, as pleasant as great; here said to have commanded ten nations. It lieth on the north of Galilee, in a valley beyond Antelibanus, six short days' journey from Jerusalem.

Ver. 219. *Sabaste.*] Samaria, the sovereign city of those ten tribes which fell from the House of Judah, not much above a day's journey from Jerusalem; built by Amri on the top of a hill, presenting an admirable prospect, which he bought of Samarus, of whom it was called Samaria. The inhabitants infamous for their frequent falling from God to idolatry.

Ver. 221. *Phœnicians, who.*] The inhabitants between the great sea and Galilee (so called of Phœnix their king, the fifth in descent from Jupiter), honoured for the invention of letters.

" Phœnicians first express'd (if Fame be true)
The fix'd voice in rude figures. Memphis knew
Not yet how stream-lov'd Biblus to prepare;
But birds and beasts, carv'd out in stone, declare
Their hieroglyphic wisdom."

Lucan. l. 3.

These Cadmus, the son of Agenor, communicated to the Grecians.

Ver. 223. *Tyrus, full of luxury.*] The metropolis of Phœnicia, once sovereign of the sea, and of all the world the greatest emporium; whose beauty, commerce and riches, the parent of luxury, is by the Prophet Ezekiel most gloriously described.

Ver. 224. *Mother Sidon.*] The ancientest city of Phœnicia, built by Sida, the daughter of Belus, or rather by Sidon, the first-born of Canaan. The mother of Tyrus, for the Tyrians were a colony of the Sidonians.

Ver. 226. *Among the Syrians, those, &c.*] The Syrians would eat no fish, not only in regard of the fabulous transformation of their goddess Dercetis, but that they held it injustice to kill those creatures which did them no harm, and were fed on rather for luxury than necessity; withal, conceiving the sea to be the original and father of all that had life, and that man was engendered of a liquid substance, they adored fishes as being of their own generation and subsistence. So did they a dove, not only because their glorious Empress Semiramis carried that name, and was after, as they fable, transformed into that creature; but expressing the air by the dove, as by a fish the water; reverencing both, as comprising the nature of all things.

Ver. 229. *From Belus, whose, &c.*] From certain marishes in the valley of Acre runs the river of Belus with a tardy pace, and exonerates itself into the sea hard by Ptolemais, whose sand affordeth matter for glass, becoming fusible in the furnace. Strabo reports the like of divers places thereabout; and Josephus, speaking of this, that there is an adjoining pit, an hundred cubits in circuit, covered with sand that glistered like glass, and when carried away (for therewith they accustomed to ballast their ships) it forthwith was filled again, borne thither by winds from places adjacent. Moreover, that what mineral soever was contained therein, converted into glass, and glass there laid, again into sand.

Ver. 231. *From Arnon's banks, those, &c.*] Arnon riseth in the mountains of Arabia, and, dividing the country of the Moabites from the Ammonites, falls into the Dead Sea. By those ancient wars is meant the overthrow which Moses gave unto Og and Sihon.

Ver. 234. *Asphaltis.*] The Dead Sea, or Lake of Sodom and Gomorrah, having no egress, unless under the earth, seventy miles in length, and sixteen broad, here at large described by our author.

Ver. 237. *What over flies, &c.*] The like is written of Avernus, whereof the poetical philosopher:—

"Avernus call'd; a name impos'd of right,
In that so fatal to all birds of flight.
Which, when those airy passengers o'er-fly,
Forgetful of their wings, they fall from high
With stretch'd-out necks on earth; where earth partakes
That killing property; where lakes on lakes."
                                                Lucr. l. 6.

Ver. 250. *When she, &c.*] Lot's wife. Josephus writes that he himself had seen that statue of salt; yet extant, if Brocardus and Saligniacus, professed eye-witnesses, be to be believed.

Ver. 255. *Devout Esseans.*] A sect among the Jews, strictly preserving the worship of God, the rules of religion and justice, living on the common stock, never eating of flesh, and wholly abstaining from wine and women. They wore their apparel white and cleanly, prayed before the rising of the sun, laboured all day long for the public utility, fed in the evening with a general silence, and had their sobriety rewarded with a life long and healthful. Their chief study was the Bible, and next to that physic, taking their name from the cure of diseases. All were servants one to another. They never sware an oath, nor offered anything that had life in their sacrifice; ascribing all unto fate, and nothing to free-will. They preserved their society by the adoption of children inured to piety and labour. Their sect, though ancient, hath no known original, yet much agreeing with the discipline of the Pythagoreans.

Ver. 274. *The first unleavened bread.*] Eaten with the Paschal Lamb at the Israelites' departing out of Egypt: the ceremonies used therein are at large delivered by Moses.

Ver. 275. *She never would retain.*] The liberty they lost in the Babylonian captivity was never absolutely recovered; for the most part under the Persians, Grecians, Egyptians, or Syrians (although in the reign of the Asmones they had the face of a kingdom, yet maintained with perpetual bloodshed) after governed by the Idumeans, and lastly by the Romans; often rebelling, and as often suppressed.

Ver. 278. *Horned Hammon's temple.*] Jupiter Hammon, which signifies Sand, because his temple stood in the Lybian deserts; with such difficulty visited by Alexander. Or rather, being the same with Ham, the son of Noah, from whom idolatry had her original, who usually wore the carved head of a ram on his helmet, whereupon his idol was so fashioned. But Jupiter Hammon is also taken for the sun, Hammah signifying heat in the Hebrew; and because the year beginneth at his entrance into Aries, he therefore was carved with ram's horns.

Ver. 281. *Built his proud city.*] Alexandria in Egypt, built by Alexander the Great upon a promontory near the isle of Pharos, so directed, as they write, by Homer in a vision.

Ver. 282. *To their old prison, Babylon.*] Not all the Jews returned with Zorobbabel, but remained at Babylon, and by the favour of succeeding princes planted thereabout their colonies, grew a great nation, observing their ancient rites and religion. These were called Babylonian Jews, to whom not a few of their countrymen fled from the troubles of their country.

Ver. 283. *To freezing Taurus, &c.*] The greatest mountain of the world, which changeth its name according to the countries through which it extendeth; that part properly so called, which divideth Pamphilia and Cilicia from the lesser Armenia and Cappadocia, whither many of the Jews were retired.

Ver. 284. *And Tiber now, &c.*] Rome, the empress of cities, adorning the banks of Tiber, to which the ocean then yielded obedience.

THE SECOND ACT.

PETER.

YOU offspring of bloodthirsty Romulus,
Foes to sweet peace, to our Great God,
and us,
And you profaner sacrificers, who
With subtil mischief guiltless blood pursue;
Since you would not refuse to bind the hands   5
Of Innocence, on me impose your bands:
Seize on the guilty; he who hath refus'd
His Lord and Master, by himself accus'd.
The ills yet suffer'd, I deserve to bear
For looking on; what follows, for my fear.   10
You need no torches to subdue the night's
Dark shades to find me; no stern satellites
Drawn from the Temple, nor with Romans join
To act one sin; nor spend your sacred coin
In salary to such a Guide as may   15
With a perfidious kiss his Lord betray.
This head I give you freely; hither haste:
No sudden whirlwinds shall your bodies cast
On trembling earth. Behold, I with my hands
Behind me bound, implore your dire commands,   20
And run to meet your stripes. Are you now prone
To melting pity? Will you punish none

But with injustice? Is your fury slow,
Unless to those who no offences know?
We both alike have impiously transgrest: 25
You in not punishing a fault confest;
And I who have the Living Lord denied.
Just judges of a life so sanctified,
To whom suborned witnesses have sold
Their damned perjuries, a wretch behold, 30
And hear his crime: My country Galilee,
To follow Christ, I left, both land and sea;
Son to the Thunderer, His only Heir,
From Heav'n sent by His Father to repair
And rule th' affairs of mortals: This is He, 35
Whom you have bound, Who must his country free.
Rebellious vassals, you have doom'd your King.
I know the impious race from whence you spring,
Your savage manners, cruel ancestors,
Whom Nature, as her greatest curse, abhors. 40
Such, when the trembling boy his brethren's hands,
Their truculent aspects, and servile bands
Beheld; though privy to a better fate,
Whose providence was to reward their hate:
Soon after, call'd to Nile's sev'n-channell'd flood, 45
He famine from both lands expell'd with food.
So your seditious fathers mutinied
At Sina's rocks, against their sacred Head:
And there the food of angels loath'd, which fell
From heav'n in show'rs: besotted Israel 50
Egypt and servitude preferr'd above
The tents of Moses and their country's love.
What numbers, with prophetic raptures fill'd,
Have you, and yet not unrevenged, kill'd!
Memphis, devouring deserts, civil wars, 55
Oft foreign yokes, Assyrian conquerors,
Great Pompey's eagles, sacred rites profan'd,
   Your Temple sack'd, with slaughter'd Levites
      stain'd;

A TRAGEDY.

Are all forgot? Yet worse attend your hate.
O that I were the minister of fate! 60
I then would tear your guilty buildings down,
And in a crimson sea their ruins drown.
Witness you groves, late conscious of our cares,
Where Christ with tears pour'd forth His funeral
  pray'rs,
How I revenge pursu'd; and with their blood 65
Would have augmented Cedron's murmuring
  flood:
But He, for Whom I struck, reprov'd the blow,
And, following His own precept, cur'd His foe.
For Malchus, rushing on in front of all,
Perceiving part of his, with-out him, fall, 70
Search'd with his flaming brand: the bleeding ear
Seen on the earth, revenge subdu'd his fear;
Who loudly roaring shook his threaten'd bands,
And straight encounter'd those all-healing Hands.
They to his head that ornament restor'd, 75
And benefits for injuries afford.
But O blind mischief! I, who gave the wound,
Am left at large; and He, Who heal'd it, bound.
O Peter, canst thou yet forbear to throw
Thy body on the weapons of the foe? 80
If thou would'st vindicate thy Lord, begin
First with thyself, and punish thy own sin.
Thou that dar'st menace armies, thou that art
Fierce as a Midian tiger, of a heart
Invincible, nor knows what 'tis to dread, 85
With Fortune, at the first encounter, fled.
A fugitive, a rebel; one that hath
All crimes committed in this breach of faith.
Who tow'ring hopes on his own strength erects,
Nor the self-flatt'ring mind's deceit suspects, 90
But his vain virtue trust, let him in me
The sad example of his frailty see:

From slippery heights how pronely mortals slide,
Their heady errors punishing their pride.
What can I add to these misdeeds of mine,   95
Who have defil'd the water, bread, and wine,
With my abhorr'd defection? O, could I
Those lips pollute with wilful perjury,
But newly-feasted with that Sacred Food,
Presenting His torn Flesh, and pour'd-out Blood!
O Piety! for this, thou renegate,   101
Did Jesus wash thy flying feet of late?
Not Jordan with two heads, whose waters roll
From snow-top Libanus, can cleanse thy soul;
Not thou, Callirhoe; nor that ample lake,   105
From whose forsaken shore my birth I take.
Could'st thou blue Nereus, in whose troubled deep
Nile's sev'n large mouths their foaming currents
    steep?
Or that Red Sea, whose waves in rampires stood,
While our forefathers pass'd the parted flood?   110
These purging streams from thy own springs
    must flow.
Repentance, why are thy complaints so slow?
Raise storms of sighs; let tears in torrents fall,
And on thy blushing cheeks deep furrows gall.
O so! run freely: beat thy stubborn breast: 115
Here spend thy rage; these blows become thee best.
This, wretched Cephas, for thy crimes I owe:
What can I for my injured Lord bestow?
My deeds and suff'rings disproportion'd are,
Nor must they in an equal sorrow share.   120
Should this night ever last, to propagate
Increasing sorrows, till subdu'd by Fate,
My penitent soul this wasted flesh forsake,
Yet can my guilt no reparation make.
Swoll'n eyes, now weep you? then you should
    have wept,   125

Besprinkled my devotion, and have kept
That holy watch, when interdicted sleep
Your drowsy lids did in his Lethe steep.
You should have dropp'd my brains into a flood,
Before He at that dire tribunal stood ;   130
Ere, thrice abjur'd, on me His looks he threw;
Or ere th' accusing bird of dawning crew.
Where shall I hide me ? In what dungeon may
My troubled soul avoid the woful day ?
Fly quickly to some melancholy cave,   135
In whose dark entrails thou may'st find a grave
To bury thee alive : there waste thy years
In cherish'd sorrow, and unwitness'd tears.

   Pontius Pilate: Caiaphas.

ARPEIAN Jove ; Mars, great Quirinus'
 sire ;
 You household gods, snatch'd from
  Troy's funeral fire,   140
With greater zeal ador'd ; when shall I pay
My vows ? my off'rings on your altars lay ?
And see those roofs which top the clouds, the
 beams
With burnish'd gold inchas'd, and blazing gems ?
Those theatres, which ring with their applause 145
Who on the conquer'd world impose their laws ?
And thee, the triple earth's impetuous guide,
Great-soul'd Tiberius, whether thou reside
On Tiber's banks, ador'd by grateful Rome,
Ambitious of his residence, for whom   150
She gave the world ; or Capræ, much renown'd
For soft delights, impoverish the long-gown'd ?
Far from my friends, far from my native soil,
I here in honourable exile toil,
To curb a people whom the gods disclaim :   155
Who cover under the usurpéd name

Of piety, their hate to all mankind;
Condemn the world; in their own vices blind;
And with false grounded fear abjure for One,
All those immortals which the heav'ns inthrone.
Their only law is to renounce all laws :   161
Their error, which from others hatred draws,
Fomenting their own discord, still provokes
Their spirits to rebellion, who their yokes
Have oft attempted to shake off; though they   165
More easily are subdu'd than taught to obey..
Clear justice, sincere faith, bear witness you
With how much grief our swords the Hebrews slew:
But such as stubborn and inhuman are,
Unless they suffer, would enforce a war: 170
And reason urgeth those who sceptres bear,
Against their nature, oft to prove severe.
I go to question what these prelates would,
Since they forbear to enter, lest they should
(Their feast so near) with my unhallow'd floor 175
Their feet pollute. Who's this, by such a pow'r
In shackles led? How reverent His aspect!
How full of awe! Those looks no guilt detect.
Thou Caiaphas, of Solyma the prime,
And prince of priests, relate th' imputed crime. 180

CAIAPHAS.

Great guardian of the Roman peace, whom we
Next Cæsar honour; to be doom'd by thee,
Our Senate brings th' Infection of these times :
Whom we accuse of no suggested crimes.
Those holy rites which grave antiquity   185
First introducéd, since defended by
A long descent, this Innovator sought
To abolish, and a new religion taught.
Nor fearing the recess of God's own seat,
The Temple's ruin sings, and roof replete   190.

A TRAGEDY. 441

With the full Deity: disturbs the feast
Of the Seventh Day, design'd for sacred rest.
Those laws rejects which Moses' pen reveal'd,
Ev'n those by God with dreadful thunder seal'd.
Nor so content; with Heav'n His fury wars,   195
Aspires that throne, and tramples on the stars.
Who styles Himself, though of ignoble birth,
His Only Son, Who made both heav'n and earth.
This, death must expiate: he hath judg'd His
  cause,
Who writ in leaves of marble our ten laws.   200

PILATE.

When wrath, the nurse of war, and thirst of gold
Destructive arts produc'd, the better soul'd
No peace nor safety found, enforc'd to bear:
Life, of itself infirm, through common fear
Into societies the scatter'd drew,   205
Who by united forces potent grew:
Entrenchéd cities with high walls immur'd;
But more by well-digested laws secur'd:
The crime and punishment proportion kept;
And wrongs, like wolves, on their first authors
  leapt: 210
Justice from each offence example took;
And his own weapon the delinquent strook:
Spoil seiz'd on rapine, blood drew blood; deterr'd
From doing that which they to suffer fear'd.
But more than human plagues attend on those   215
Who God provoke: He prosecutes His foes
With sure revenge. Why should those Hands
  which tear
The clouds with thunder, shake the world with
  fear,
Their wrath to man resign? The impious find
Their scourge: the terror of th' astonish'd mind   220

Affrights their peace : who feel what they deny,
And fear an unbelieved Deity.
One day no period to his torment gives,
To tremble at the name of death he lives,
Still apprehending what than death is worse,   225
Long life awarded to prolong his curse.
But if He have your laws infring'd, be you
Yourselves the judges, and His guilt pursue.

CAIAPHAS.

Although those ancient laws, which now remain
Among us, we acknowledge to retain   230
From Rome's free bounty; yet to you 'tis known,
Our curbéd pow'r can death inflict on none.
You, to whom Cæsar's fortunes recommend
His rods and axes, sacred rule defend.
This guilty wretch, Whose practices we fear,   235
Of late His place of birth forsaking, where
The sea is honour'd with Tiberius' name,
With troops of clients to this city came.
Who seeds of war among the vulgar sows :
With what injustice Roman arms impose   240
Their tribute on a nation ever free.
With magic charms and Stygian compact, He
Attracts belief : denies the dead their rest,
Of those unenvied mansions dispossest
By wicked spells. These prodigies delude   245
The novelty-affecting multitude :
Whom for their Lord their loud hosannas greet,
And strew the noble palm beneath His feet.
Embolden'd by these arts, He, as His own
By birth, aspires to David's ancient throne.   250
When Rome, provok'd by His rebellion, shall
Arm her just grief, we by the sword must fall,
Our city sink in flames, our country lie
Depopulated. But since one must die

A TRAGEDY.

To save the general, sentenc'd by thy breath, 255
Let Him redeem His nation with His death.

PILATE.

Such doubtful causes grave advice require:
Here, if you please, attend; while I retire.
The prisoner to the soldiers' care commit,
On Whom this day we will in judgment sit. 260

CHORUS OF JEWISH WOMEN.

YOU lofty towers of Solyma,
Thou ancient throne of sov'reign sway:
To thee the conquer'd tribute paid,
From th' Isthmus, crown'd with ebon shade,
To great Euphrates' trembling streams, 265
Arabians, scorch'd by Phœbus' beams.
Th' admiring queen, wing'd with thy fame,
From her black-peopled empire came.
Great kings, ambitious of thy love,
To join with thee in friendship strove. 270
Those who Canopus' sceptre bore,
Those monarchs who the sun adore,
And o'er the wealthy Orient reign:
Sarrana, sov'reign of the main.
Now, ah! a miserable thrall! 275
O nothing, but a prey to all!
This land, t' one God once chastely wed,
How often hath she chang'd her head,
Since they our temple's ruin'd pride
With bad presage re-edified! 280
Since those, in foreign bondage born,
Did with their servile fates return!
On us Antiochus' guilt reflects:
Our father's sins sit on our necks.

What durst that wicked age not do, 285
Which could those altars naked view,
Oft flaming with celestial fire?
Provoking Heav'n's deserved ire
With their adult'rate sacrifice?
For this did ours so highly prize 290
Th' Ionian gods, by mortals made,
And incense to those idols paid?
Since when th' accurs'd their brothers slew;
Wives, less malicious poison brew;
Sons fall by mothers: we have known 295
That which will be believ'd by none.
Twice vanquishéd by Roman arms;
Twice have their conquerors our harms
Remov'd for greater: fortune's change
To our proud masters prov'd as strange. 300
Yet this no less our grief provokes,
Our kindred bear divided yokes:
One part by Roman bondage wrung;
The other two by brothers, sprung
From savage Idumæans, whom 305
Our fathers have so oft o'ercome.
O thou the Hope, the only One,
Of our distress, and ruin'd throne;
Of Whom, with a prophetic tongue,
To Judah dying Jacob sung: 310
The crownéd muse on ivory lyre,
His breast inflam'd with holy fire,
This oft foretold: that Thou shouldst free
The people consecrate to Thee;
That Thou, triumphing, shouldst revoke 315
Sweet peace, then never to be broke;
When freed Judea should obey
One Lord, and all affect His sway.
O when shall we behold Thy face,
So often promis'd to our race? 320

If prophets, who have won belief
By our mishaps and flowing grief,
Of joyful change as truly sung,
Thy absence should not now be long.
Thee, by Thy virtue, we entreat;   325
The temple's veil, the mercy-seat;
That Name, by which our fathers sware,
Which in our vulgar speech we dare
Not utter, to compassionate
Thy kindred's tears, and ruin'd state.   330
Haste, to our great redemption, haste,
O Thou Most Holy! and at last
Bless with Thy presence, that we may
To Thee our vows devoutly pay.

ANNOTATIONS ON THE SECOND ACT.

VERSE 1. *Blood-thirsty Romulus.*] The original of the race and name of the Romans, who laid the walls of Rome in the blood of his brother Remus.

Ver. 15. *To such a Guide, &c.*] It was a custom among the eastern nations, and not relinquished by many at this day, for men to kiss one another in their salutations; so did the Romans, until interdicted by Tiberius. With the Jews it was a pledge of peace and amity, used also to their lords and princes by way of homage and acknowledged subjection, as perfidious Judas did here to his Master.

Ver. 55. *Memphis.*] By this is meant the Egyptian servitude; Memphis of old, the chief city in Egypt.

Ver. 55. *Devouring deserts.*] All the Israelites that came out of Egypt perished in the deserts, but Joshua and Caleb.

Ver. 55. *Civil wars.*] As between the tribe of Benjamin and the rest of the tribes, the Jews and Israelites; Israelites against Israelites, and Jews against Jews. Discord threw her snakes among the Asmones; nor had Herod's posterity better success.

Ver. 56. *Oft foreign yokes.*] Often subdued by their neighbours, and delivered by their judges and princes.

Ver. 56. *Assyrian conquerors.*] Who sacked Jerusalem, destroyed the temple which was built by Solomon, led their king captive, and their whole nation, unto Babylon.

Ver. 57. *Great Pompey's eagles.*] Pompey, who bore the Roman eagle on his standard, took Jerusalem and the temple by force (yet would not meddle with the treasure nor sacred utensils) subdued the Jews, and made them tributaries to the Romans.

Ver. 57. *Sacred rites profaned.*] Who entered the Sanctum Sanctorum with his followers, and profaned the religion of the place by beholding that which was to be seen but by the high priest only.

Ver. 58. *The temple sacked, with blood, &c.*] He slew twelve thousand Jews within the walls of the temple.

Ver. 66. *Cedron.*] This brook or torrent runs through the vale of Jehoshaphat, between Mount Olivet and the city, close by the Garden of Gethsemane, where Christ was betrayed.

Ver. 103. *Not Jordan with two, &c.*] See the note upon ver. 195, Act I.

Ver. 105. *Callirhoë.*] A city in the tribe of Reuben, so called of her beautiful springs, where from a rock two neighbour fountains gush out as from the breasts of a woman, the one of hot but sweet water, the other of cold and bitter, which joining together make a pleasant bath, salubrious for many diseases, and flow from thence into the lake of Asphaltis. Herod in his sickness repaired to this place, but finding no help, and despairing of life, removed to Jericho, where he died.

Ver. 105. *That ample lake.*] The Sea of Galilee, by which Peter was born.

Ver. 107. *Blue Nereus, &c.*] Nereus is taken for the sea in general, but here for the Egyptian, into which Nilus dischargeth his waters by seven currents, the fresh water keeping together, and changing the colour of the salt, far further into the sea than the shore from thence can be discerned.

Ver. 128. *Lethe.*] A river of Africa, passing by Bernice, and running into the Mediterranean Sea near the promontory of the Syrtes. It hath that name from Oblivion, because those who drunk thereof forgot whatsoever they had formerly done. Of this, Lucan:—

" Where silent Lethe glides : this (as they tell)
Draws her Oblivion from the veins of Hell."

So feigned, because of the oblivion which is in death, as allegorically for that of sleep.

Ver. 139. *Tarpeian Jove.*] Tarpeius is a mountain in Rome, taking that name from the vestal virgin Tarpea, who betrayed her father's fort to the Sabines upon promise to receive what they wore on their left arms for her reward, she meaning their golden bracelets, which they not only gave, but threw their shields upon her (a part of the bargain), and so pressed her to death, who buried her in the place, since called the Capitol, where Jupiter had his temple.

Ver. 139. *Mars, great Quirinus' sire.*] Romulus was called Quirinus of his spear; or for his uniting the two nations of the Cures and Romans. as the son of Mars, in that so strenuous a soldier. Plutarch writes that he was begotten by his uncle Æmulius, who counterfeiting Mars disguised in armour, ravished his mother Ilia, not only to satisfy his lust but to procure her destruction, as the heir to his elder brother, the law condemning a defiled vestal to be buried alive.

Ver. 140. *You household gods, snatched, &c.*] Penates, which Æneas saved from burning at the sack of Troy, and brought them with him into Italy, supposing that from them they received their flesh, their life, and understanding.

Ver. 151. *Capræ.*] A little island in the Tyrrhen Sea, and in the sight of Naples, naturally walled about with upright cliffs, and having but one passage into it. Infamous for the cruelties and lusts of Tiberius; who, retiring thither from the affairs of the commonwealth, sent from thence his mandates of death; polluting the place with all variety of uncleanness, whereupon it was called the island of secret lusts, and he Caprenius, conversing there with magicians and soothsayers; whereof the satire, speaking of Sejanus:—

"The prince's tutor glorying to be named;
Sitting in caves of Capræ with defamed
Chaldeans." *Juv. Sat.* 10.

Ver. 152. *The long-gowned.*] The gown was a garment peculiar to the Romans, by which they were distinguished from other nations, as of what quality among themselves by the wool and colour, fashion and trimming, insomuch as they were called Togati, whereof Virgil in the person of Jupiter

THE SECOND ACT.

"Curst Juno, who sea, earth, and heaven above
With her distemper tires, shall friendly prove;
And join with us in gracing the long-gown'd
And lordly Romans, still with conquest crown'd."
Aen. l. 1.

Ver. 157. *Their hate to all, &c.*] The Jews with the hate of an enemy detested all other nations, would neither eat with them, nor lodge in their houses, but avoided the stranger as a pollution. Proud in their greatest poverty; calling themselves the elect of God; boasting of their country, their religion, and ancient families; in their conversation austere and respectless. So full of jealous envy, that, by a decree in the reign of Hircanus and Aristobulus, such suffered the dreadful censure of a curse who instructed their sons in the Grecian disciplines, and much regretted that the laws of Moses were translated into a profane language by the command of Philadelphus, expressing their grief by an annual fast, which they kept on the eighth day of the month Teveth.

Ver. 159. *Abjure for one, &c.*] Pilate accuseth them here for their piety, who, after the Captivity, as much detested idolatry as they affected it before; who could not be compelled by their conquerors to worship the images of Tiberius Cæsar, which Pilate brought into the city, but was forced to carry them away upon their refusal. Caius not long after commanded that the statues of the gods should be erected in their temple, menacing, if they should refuse it, their utter subversion. But his death prevented their ruin, who before had made their protestation that they would rather suffer the general destruction of themselves and their city than suffer such an abomination so repugnant to their law and religion.

Ver. 168. *With how much grief our swords, &c.*] Josephus mentions one slaughter only, which Pilate, as then, had made of the Jews, and that about the drawing of water by conduits into the sacred treasury, which divers thousands of the Jews tumultuarily resisted. Pilate environed them with his soldiers, disguised in popular garments, who privately armed, fell upon the naked people, and, by the slaughter of a number, appeased the mutiny.

Ver. 234. *Rods and axes.*] Borne before the Roman

consuls, pretors, and governors of provinces, bound together in bundles, to inform the magistrate that he should not be too swift in execution, nor unlimited; but that in the unbinding thereof he might have time to deliberate, and perhaps to alter his sentence; that some are to be corrected with rods, and others cut off with axes, according to the quality of their offences.

Ver. 242. *Stygian.*] Styx is a fountain of Arcadia, whose waters are so deadly that they presently kill whatsoever drinks thereof; so corrodiating, that they can only be contained in the hoof of a mule. This, in regard of the dire effects, was feigned by the poets to be a river in hell.

Ver. 254. *Since one must die, &c.*] Caiaphas prophesied, being then the high priest, though not of the house of Aaron. He was thrown out of his office by Lucius Vitellius, who succeeded Pilate, and Jonathan, the son of Annas, placed in his room; when distracted with melancholy and desperation, he received his death from his own hands.

Ver. 361. *Solyma.*] So called by the Grecians, as by the Hebrews Salem; and when David had taken it from the Jebusites, Jerusalem, which is as much as Jebusalem, turning B into R for the better harmony: called after the building of the Temple Hierosolyma by the Greeks of Hieron, which signifies a temple in their language.

Ver. 264. *From th' isthmus.*] This isthmus lies between Egypt and the bottom of the Red Sea, from whence to Euphrates David extended his conquests, enforcing all the Arabians to become his tributaries. Who also overthrew the King of Sophona hard by the eruption of Tigris, overcame the Mesopotamians, the King of Damascus, and drew that city, with all Syria, under his obedience, having before subdued the neighbouring nations.

Ver. 267. *Th' admiring queen, &c.*] Josephus makes her Queen of Ethiopia, and to have bestowed on Solomon that precious plant of balsamum which he after planted in Engaddi; but this grew in Canaan in the days of Jacob, who sent a present thereof, among other fruits of that country, into Egypt. The Ethiopian emperors glory in their descent from Solomon by this queen, in regard whereof they greatly favour the Jewish nation. They have a city called Saba, which lies on the west side of the Arabian

Gulf. But by the presents which she brought, and vicinity of the country, it is more probable that she came from Saba, the principal city of Arabia the Happy.

Ver. 271. *Canopus sceptre, &c.*] Kings of Egypt, of Canopus, a principal city, which stood on that branch of Nilus which is next to Alexandria, taking that name from Menelaus his pilot, there buried by his shipwrecked master.

Ver. 272. *Those monarchs, &c.*] Chaldean monarchs: Babylon, the seat of their empire; who, as the Persians, adored the sun under the name of " Mithra."

Ver. 274. *Sarrana.*] Tyrus: so called in that it was built on a rock: the Arabians pronouncing Scar for Sar, from whence the Tyrian purple takes the name of scarlet:—

" He cities sacks, and houses fills with groans;
To lie on scarlet, drink in precious stones."
Virg. Geor. l. 2.

Not only Josephus, but the Scriptures, make often mention of the ancient amity between the Jews and Tyrians.

Ver. 277. *This land, &c.*] See the note upon v. 275, act 1.

Ver. 283. *Antiochus' guilt.*] Antiochus Epiphanes; who abrogated their law, and by threatenings and tortures enforced the Jews to idolatry, polluting their altar with sacrificed swine.

Ver. 291. *Ionian gods.*] The gods of Greece: Antiochus being of a Grecian family, and zealous in their superstitions.

Ver. 293. *Their brothers slew, &c.*] Aristobulus, the first that wore a crown of the race of the Asmones, upon a false suspicion, by the machination of Salome the Queen, caused his valiant and affectionate brother Antigonus to be treacherously murdered; who before had imprisoned the rest of his brethren, and famished his mother. After the desperate death of Aristobulus, Alexander his brother was removed from a prison to a throne: who slew his third brother out of a vain suspicion of his aspiring to the kingdom. To conclude, from the first King of the Asmones to the last of the Herods, no history is so fruitful in examples of unnatural cruelties.

Ver. 297. *Twice vanquish'd, &c.*] Pompey was the first of the Romans that subdued the Jews: neither were the

Romans expulsed by any foreign prince, but until this time maintained their government. It must then be meant by their expulsion of one another in their civil wars: Julius Cæsar vanquishing Pompey; Mark Antony being his lieutenant in Syria (who gave a great part of the territories of the Jews to Cleopatra); after absolute lord of the eastern parts of the Roman empire; in the end overthrown and deprived of all by Augustus.

Ver. 303. *One part by Roman, &c.*] Judæa reduced into a Roman province by Pompey, and then governed by Pontius Pilate.

Ver. 304. *The other two by brothers, &c.*] Philip and Antipas (called also Herod) sons to Herod the Great; the one Tetrarch of Iturea, a country which lies at the foot of Libanus, and the other of Galilee, to whom Agrippa succeeded (the son of Aristobulus slain by his father Herod) with the title of a king bestowed by Cæsar.

Ver. 305. *From savage Idumæans.*] Antipater, the father of Herod, was an Idumæan; who, in the contention between the two brethren Hircanus and Aristobulus about the kingdom, took part with Hircanus, and grew so powerful, that he made a way for his son to the sovereignty, though he himself was prevented by poison.

Ver. 327. *That Name.*] Jehovah.

THE THIRD ACT.

JUDAS. CAIAPHAS.

OU who preserve your pure integrity,
O you whose crimes transcend not credit, fly
Far from my presence; whose en-venom'd sight
Pollutes the guilty! Thou, who wrong and right
Distinctly canst discern; whose gentle breast 5
All faith hath not abandon'd, but art blest
With children, brothers, friends; nor hast declin'd
The sweet affections of a pious mind;
Shut up the winding entry of thine ear,
Nor let the world of such a bargain hear. 10
A sin so horrible should be to none
Besides the desperate contractors known.
Where's now that mitred chief? where that dire train
Of sacrificers, worthy to be slain
On their own altars? I have found my curse:
The sun, except myself, sees nothing worse.
Hear, without hire; O hear the too well-known:
If you seek for a witness, I am one
That can the truth reveal: or would you find
A villain? Here's a self-accusing mind. 20
That Sacred Life, O most immaculate!
More than my masters! to your deadly hate

Have I betray'd: discharge my hands I may,
Although not of the guilt, yet of the prey.
Receive the gift you gave: a treachery   25
Second to mine, you may of others buy.

CAIAPHAS.

If thou accuse thyself of such a sin
Deservedly, thou hast a court within
That will condemn thee. Thy offences be
No crimes of ours: our consciences are free.   30
Nor shall the sacred treasury receive
The price of blood. Thee to thy fate we leave.

JUDAS.

Is this the doctrine of your piety,
To approve the crime, yet hate the hire? O fly,
Fly, wretch, unto the altar, and pollute   35
The temple with thy sin's accursèd fruit.
Nor will I for myself with hopeless pray'r
Solicit heav'n, lost in my own despair;
But God's stern justice urge, that we, who were
Join'd in the guilt, may equal vengeance bear.   40
Nor shall I in my punishment prove slow:
Behold, your leader will before you go;
'Tis fit you follow; to those silent deeps,
Those horrid shades, where sorrow never sleeps.
Thou great Director of the rolling stars,   45
Unless Thou idly lookst on men's affairs,
And vainly we Thy brutish thunder fear,
Why should Thy land so dire a monster bear?
Or the sun not retire, and yet behold?
If those Thy fearful punishments of old   50
Require belief, in one unite them all:
Let seas in cataracts from meteors fall,
Afford no shore, but swallow in their brine;
That so the world's first ruin may prove mine.

Let melting stars their sulph'rous surfeit shed, 55
And all the heav'nly fires fall on my head.
And thou, O injur'd earth, thy jaws extend,
That I may to th' infernal shades descend:
Less cause had Thy revenge, when she the five
Enrag'd conspirators devour'd alive. 60
Those evils which amaz'd the former times,
Thy fury hath consum'd on smaller crimes.
O slow Revenger of His injuries,
And He Thy Son! some fearful death devise,
Unknown and horrid: or shall I pursue 65
My own offence, and act what Thou shouldst do?
You legions of heav'n's exiles, you who take
Revenge on mortals for the crimes you make,
Why troop you thus about me? Or what need
These terrors? Is my punishment decreed 70
In hell already? Furies, now I come.
In your dark dungeons what more horrid Rome
Shall now devour me? Must I to that place,
Where the curs'd father[1] of a wicked race
Your scourges feels? who, when the world was new, 75
And but possess'd by four, his brother slew.
Or where that faithless prince[2] blasphemes, than all
His host more eminent; who, lest his fall
Should honour to his enemies afford,
Made way for hated life with his own sword? 80
He most affects me who his father's chair
Usurp'd; when caught by his revenging hair,
He[3] lost the earth and life: the way he led
T' avoided death, my willing feet shall tread.
Master, I fly to anticipate the event 85
Of my foul crime with equal punishment.

---

[1] Cain.   [2] Saul.   [3] Absalom.

PONTIUS PILATE. THE JEWS.

HORROR distracts my sense: irresolute
Whether I should break silence, or sit
mute.
Envy th' Accus'd condemns, Whom justice clears.
I must confess, persuaded by my fears, 90
Lest I this state and people should incense,
I wish'd they could have prov'd that great offence.
Yet whatsoever they enforc'd of late,
No fault of His reveal'd, but their own hate.
His silence was a vanquishing reply. 95
Who for detecting their false piety
(Whose supercilious looks, with fasting pale,
Close avarice and proud ambition veil)
Is by their arts made guilty: One that slights
The God they adore, and violates His rites. 100
From hence those many-nam'd offences spring,
And His aspiring to become their King.
Can those poor fishers of that inland sea,
And women, following Him from Galilee,
So great a spirit in their Leader raise, 105
That Rome should fear, whom all the world
obeys?
Yet He avers His Kingdom is unknown,
Nor of this world; and bows to Cæsar's throne.
Prov'd by th' event: for when the vulgar bound
His yielding Hands, they no resistance found. 110
But His endowments, zealous in defence
Of clouded truth, their mortal hate incense.
Follow'd by few, who like affections bear,
And with belief their Master's doctrine hear.
If true, He may speak freely; nor must die 115
For ostentation, though He broach a lie.
But if distracted, that's a punishment
Ev'n to itself, and justice doth prevent.

A TRAGEDY.

He whom this annual solemnity
Hath now invited to the temple by 120
His father built, whose kingdom borders on
The land ennobled by Agenor's throne,
Of these stupendous acts by rumour spread
Could fix no faith, though in his city bred.
To laughter doom'd, his rival Herod scorn'd, 125
And sent Him back in purple robes adorn'd.
Th' implacable now far more fiercely bent
To prosecute the twice-found Innocent :
Perhaps afraid lest they their own should lose,
Unless they Him of forgéd guilt accuse. 130
But when revenge doth once the mind engage,
O how it raves, lost to all sense but rage!
No lioness, late of her whelps bereft,
With wilder fury prosecutes the theft.
O shame! through fear I sought to shield the right 135
With honest fraud, and justice steal by sleight :
As when the labouring bark, too weak to stem
The boist'rous tide, obliquely cuts the stream.
They have an ancient custom, if we may
Believe the Jews, derivéd from that day 140
When the deliver'd sons of Israel
Fled from those banks whose floods in summer swell—
That ever when the vernal moon shall join
Her silver orb, and in full lustre shine,
They should some one release, to gratify 145
The people, by their law condemn'd to die.
Now, hoping to have freed the Innocent,
The violent priests my clemency prevent :
Who urge the heady vulgar to demand
One Barabbas ; a thief, who had a hand 150
In ev'ry murder, hot with human blood.
How little it avails us to be good !

CHRIST'S PASSION.

Preposterous favour! through the hate they bear
His guiltless soul, their votes the guilty clear.
And now my wife's not idle dreams perplex   155
My struggling thoughts, which all this night did vex
Her troubled slumbers; who conjures me by
All that is holy, all the gods, that I
Should not the laws of justice violate
To gratify so undeserv'd a hate.   160
For this shall I the Hebrew fathers slight,
Th' endeavours of a nation so unite,
Committed to my charge? Shall I, for One
Poor abject, forfeit all the good I have done?
These pester'd walls all Jewry now enfold;   165
The houses hardly can their strangers hold,
Sent from all parts to this Great Festival:
What if the vulgar to their weapons fall?
Who knows the end, if once the storm begin?
Sure I, their judge, egregious praise should win 170
By troubling of the public peace. Shall I
Then render Him to death? Impiety!
For what offence? Is his offence not great,
Whose innovation may a war beget?
Lest empire suffer, they who sceptres bear   175
Oft make a crime, and punish what they fear.
One hope remains: our soldiers the Free-born,
And yet by our command, with whips have torn.
A sight so full of pity may assuage
The swiftly-spreading fire of popular rage.   180
Look on this spectacle! His arms all o'er
With lashes gall'd, deep dy'd in their own gore!
His sides exhausted! all the rest appears
Like that fictitious scarlet which He wears!
And for a crown, the wreathéd thorns enfold   185
His bleeding brows! With grief His grief behold!

A TRAGEDY.

JEWS.
Away with Him : from this contagion free
Th' infected earth, and nail Him on a tree.

PILATE.
What, crucify your King?

JEWS.
      Dominion can
No rival brook. His rule, a law to man,   190
Whom Rome adores we readily obey,
And will admit of none but Cæsar's sway.
He Cæsar's right usurps who hopes to ascend
The Hebrew throne. Thy own affairs intend.
Dost thou discharge thy master's trust, if in   195
Thy government a precedent begin
So full of danger, tending to the rape
Of majesty? Shall treason thus escape?

PILATE.
The tumult swells: the vulgar and the great
Join in their votes with contributed heat.   200
Whose whisp'rings such a change of murmur raise
As when the rising wind's first fury strays
'Mong wave-beat rocks, when gath'ring clouds
   deform
The face of heav'n, whose wrath begets a storm:
The fearful pilot then distrusts the skies,   205
And to the nearest port for refuge flies.
To these rude clamours they mine ears inure:
Such sharp diseases crave a sudden cure.
You my attendants, hither quickly bring
Spot-purging water from the living spring.   210
Thou liquid crystal, from pollution clear,
And you, my innocent hands, like record bear,
On whom these cleansing streams so purely run,
I voluntarily have nothing done.

Nor am I guilty, though He guiltless die : 215
Yours is the crime; His blood upon you lie.

JEWS.

Rest thou secure. If His destruction shall
Draw down celestial vengeance, let it fall
Thick on our heads, in punishment renew,
And ever our dispersèd race pursue. 220

PILATE.

Then I, from this tribunal, mounted on
Embellish'd marble, judgment's awful throne,
Thus censure : Lead Him to the cross, and by
A servile death let Judah's King there die.

CHORUS OF JEWISH WOMEN. JESUS.

WE all deplore Thy miseries ; 225
For Thee we beat our breasts ; our eyes
In bitter tears their moisture shed.
If Thou be he by ravens fed,
Aloft on flaming chariot borne,
Yet wouldst to cruel lords return : 230
Or that sad bard, believ'd too late,
Who sung his country's servile fate,
Now come to sigh her destiny,
Alike unhappy, twice to die :
Or he, long nourish'd in the wood, 235
Who late in Jordan's cleansing flood
So many wash'd ; that durst reprove
A king for his incestuous love;
Slain for a dancer. If the same,
Or other of an elder fame, 240
Sent back to earth, in vices drown'd,
To raise it from that dark profound;

'Tis sure Thy sanctity exceeds,
Blaz'd by Thy virtue and Thy deeds.
O never more, ring'd with a throng   245
Of followers, shall Thy sacred tongue
Inform our actions, nor the way
To heav'n, and heav'nly joys, display!
The blind, who now the unknown light
Beholds, scarce trusting his own sight,   250
Thy gift, shall not the Giver see.
Those maladies, subdu'd by Thee,
Which pow'rful art and herbs defy,
No more Thy sov'reign touch shall fly.
Nor loaves, so tacitly increas'd,   255
Again so many thousands feast.
Thou rule of life's perfection,
By practice as by precept shown,
Late hemm'd with auditors, whose store
Encumber'd the too-narrow shore,   260
The mountains cover'd with their press,
The mountains than their people less;
For Whom our youths their garments strew,
Victorious boughs before Thee threw,
While Thou in triumph rid'st along,   265
Saluted with a joyful song:
Now see what change from fortune springs!
O dire vicissitude of things!
Betray'd, abandon'd by Thy own,
Dragg'd by Thy foes, oppos'd by none.   270
Thou hope of our afflicted state,
Thou Balm of Life, and Lord of Fate,
Not erst to such unworthy bands
Didst Thou submit Thy pow'rful Hands.
Lo, He who gave the dumb a tongue,   275
With patient silence bears His wrong!
The soldier, ah! renews his blows;
The whip new-open'd furrows shows,

Which now in angry tumours swell:
To us their wrath the Romans sell. 280
Lo, how His members flow! the smart
Confin'd to no particular part:
His stripes, which make all but one sore,
Run in confuséd streams of gore.
Art Thou the slave of Thy own fate, 285
To bear Thy torments' curséd weight?
What Arab, though he wildly stray
In wand'ring tents, and live by prey,
Or Cyclop, who no pity knows,
Would such a cruel task impose? 290
O that the fatal pressure might
Sink Thee to earth, nor weigh more light
Than death upon Thee; that Thy weak
Untwisted thread of life might break!
It were a blessing so to die: 295
But O for how great cruelty
Art Thou reserv'd! the Cross Thou now
Support'st must with Thy burden bow.

JESUS.

Daughters of Solyma, no more
My wrongs thus passionately deplore. 300
These tears for future sorrows keep:
Wives, for yourselves and children weep.
That horrid day will shortly come,
When you shall bless the barren womb,
And breast that never infant fed: 305
Then shall you wish the mountain's head
Would from his trembling basis slide,
And all in tombs of ruins hide.

CHORUS.

Alas! Thou spotless Sacrifice
To greedy death! no more our eyes 310

Shall see Thy Face! ah, never more
Shalt Thou return from death's dark shore.
Though Lazarus late at Thy call
Brake through the bars of funeral;
Rais'd from that prison to review   315
The world which then he hardly knew;
Who forthwith former sense regains;
The blood sprung in his heated veins;
His sinews supple grew, yet were
Again almost congeal'd with fear.   320
Thy followers, Sadoc, now may know
Their error from the shades below.
A few, belov'd by the Most High,
Through virtue of the Deity,
To others rarely render'd breath :   325
None ever rais'd himself from death.

ANNOTATIONS ON THE THIRD ACT.

ER. 47. *Brutish thunder.*] The philosophers will have two sorts of lightning : calling the one fatal, that is, pre-appointed and mortal; the other brutish, that is, accidental and flying at random.

Ver. 119. *He whom, &c.*] Herod Antipas, then Tetrarch of Galilee, whose father, Herod the Great, so magnificently re-edified the Temple, that the glory of the latter exceeded that of the former.

Ver. 122. *The land, &c.*] Phœnicia; the ancient kingdom of Agenor, son to Belus Priscus, who was reputed a god after his death, and honoured with temples; called Bel by the Assyrians, and Baal by the Hebrews.

Ver. 142. *Whose floods in summer swell.*] Nilus, which constantly begins to rise with the rising sun on the seventeenth of June, increasing by degrees, until it makes all the land a lake :—

"Not tied to laws of other streams, the sun
When furthest off, thy streams then poorest run :
Intemperate heaven to temper, midst of heat,
Under the burning zone, bid to grow great.
Then Nile assists the world ; lest fire should quell
The earth : and make his high-born waters swell
Against the lion's flaming jaws.——"
Lucan, l. 10.

Ver. 177. *The free-born.*] It was the custom of the Romans to punish slaves only with whips, but their children and the free with rods.

Ver. 185. *The wreathed Thorns.*] In reverence of this Crown of Thorns, which was plaited about the brows of our

ANNOTATIONS. 465

Saviour, the Christians forbare to wear any garlands on their heads in their festivals, although it were the custom of those nations among whom they lived.

Ver. 210. *Thou liquid crystal, &c.*] Pilate washed not his hands to express his innocency, as a Roman custom, but therein observing the Jewish ceremony; which was, that he who would profess himself guiltless of a suspected manslaughter should wash his hands over a heifer with her head cut off.

Ver. 218. *Let it fall, &c.*] This imprecation soon after fell upon them in all the fulness of horror; and throughout the world at this day pursues them.

Ver. 223. *Lead him to the Cross, &c.*] Pilate not only out of fear, and against his conscience, but therein infringed a law lately made by Tiberius, in the sudden execution; for by the same no offender was to suffer within ten days after his condemnation. But he met with a Nemesis; soon after turned out of his government by Vitellius for his cruelty inflicted upon the Samaritans, and sent to Rome with his accusers. But Tiberius dying before his arrival, he was banished the city by Caius; who, troubled in mind and desperate of restitution, slew himself at Vienna in France within two years after.

Ver. 228. *If thou be he, &c.*] By this place taken out of the Gospel, it appears that divers of the Jews were of the opinion of the Pythagoreans, or the Pythagoreans of theirs, concerning the transmigration of souls into other bodies.

"All alter, nothing finally decays;
Hither and thither still the spirit strays,
Guest to all bodies : out of beasts it flies
To men, from men to beasts, and never dies.
As pliant wax each new impression takes,
Fix'd to no form, but still the old forsakes;
Yet is the same : so souls the same abide,
Through various figures their reception hide."
Ovid. Met. l. 15.

Herod conceived that the soul of John the Baptist, by him wickedly murdered, was entered into the body of our Blessed Saviour. And Josephus, in his oration to his desperate companions in the Cave of Jotopata: "Those poor souls which depart from this life by the law of nature, and obediently render what from God they received, shall by Him be placed in the highest Heavens; and from thence again, after a certain revolution of time, descend by command to dwell in chaste bodies."

Ver. 239. *Slain for a dancer.*] This daughter of Herodias, as Nicephorus writes, going over a river that was frozen, fell in all but the head, which was cut off with the ice, as her body waved up and down underneath.

Ver. 321. *Sadoc.*] The author of the sect of the Sadducees. See the note upon verse 43, Act 1.

THE FOURTH ACT.

FIRST NUNCIUS.   CHORUS OF JEWISH WOMEN.
SECOND NUNCIUS.

 FROM the horrid'st act that ever fed
The fire of barbarous rage at length
   am fled;
Yet O too near! The object still
   pursues,
Floats in mine eyes, and that sad scene renews.

CHORUS.
Art thou a witness of His misery?   5
Saw'st thou the Galilean Prophet die?

FIRST NUNCIUS.
Those savages, to Scythian rocks confin'd,
Who know no God, nor virtue of the mind,
But only sense pursue; who hunger tame
With slaughter'd lives; they and their food the
   same;   10
Would this detest.
           CHORUS.
              Vain innocence! would none
Lend Him a tear? were all transform'd to stone?

FIRST NUNCIUS.
No, certainly; yet so commiserate
As pity prov'd more tyrannous than hate.
The cursèd tree with too much weight oppress'd 15
His stooping shoulders; death had now releas'd
His fainting soul; but O, the lenity
Of malice would not suffer Him to die.
Part of the load impos'd with idle scorn
On Lybian Simon, in Cyrene born, 20
To whom th' affected quiet of the fields,
Secur'd by poverty, no safety yields.
The furies of the city him surprise,
Who from the vices of the city flies;
Who bears not his own burden, that none may 25
Misdoubt, the innocent became their prey.

CHORUS.
Forthwith unmask this wretched face of woe;
All that He suffer'd, and the manner show;
What words brake from His sorrow; give thy tongue
A liberal scope: our minds not seldom long 30
To know what they abhor; nor spare our ears;
What can be heard is fancied by our fears.

FIRST NUNCIUS.
Without the city, on that side which lies
Exposéd to the boist'rous injuries
Of the cold north, to war a fatal way, 35
Infamous by our slaughters, Golgotha
Exalts his rock. No flowers there paint the field,
Nor flourishing trees refreshing shadows yield:
The ground all white, with bones of mortals spread,
Stench'd with the putrefaction of the dead, 40
And relics of unburied carcases.
Who on his agèd father's throat durst seize,
Rip up his mother's womb; who poison drest
For his own brother; or his unknown guest

Betray'd, and gave his mangled flesh for food 45
Unto the wild inhabitants of the wood;
This stage of death deserv'd: while ev'ry foul
Misdeed of theirs pursues the guilty soul.
Now when the Nazarite at this dismal place
Arrivéd, with a weak and tardy pace, 50
Lest He should die too quickly, some prefer [1]
Sweet wine mix'd with the bitter tears of myrrh.
He of the idle present hardly tastes,
But to encounter with His torments hastes.
The steel now bored His feet, whose slit veins spout 55
Like piercéd conduits; both His arms stretch'd out.
His hands fix'd with two nails. While His great soul
These tortures suffer'd, while the rising bole
Forsook the earth, and crimson torrents sprung
From His fresh wounds, He gave His grief no tongue. 60
The Cross advanc'd and fix'd; then, as more nigh
To His own heav'n, His eyes bent on the sky,
Among such never to be equall'd woes,
(Who would believe it!) pities His stern foes;
And thinks those false contrivers, those who gor'd
His flesh with wounds, more fit to be deplor'd: 66
Who ev'n their merited destruction fears;
And, falsely judg'd, the truly guilty clears.
"Father," He cries, "forgive this sin; they knew
Not what they did, nor know what now they do."
Meanwhile the soldiers, who in blood delight, 71
With hearts more hard than rocks behold this sight,
And savage rigour, never reconcil'd
To pity, all humanity exil'd;
Who, us'd to pillage, now intend their prey; 75
Nor for His death, though then a dying, stay;

---

[1] *Prefer—i. e.*proffer.

But He alive, and looking on, divide
The spoil; yet more in the spectator joy'd.
Fury in trifles sports; their scorn His poor
Yet parted garments distribute to four.   80
His inward robe, with one contexture knit,
Nor of the like division would admit,
Their votes to the dispose of lots refer,
Electing chance for their blind arbiter.
Nor was't the least of evils to behold   85
Th' ignoble partners of His pain, who old
In mischief robb'd the murder'd passengers,
Follow'd by troops, that fill'd the night with fears.
While thus they hung, none could the doubt explain,
Whether He more had sav'd than they had slain. 90
The num'rous index of each bloody deed
Now brand their lives: when those who could
    not read
At such a distance, of the next inquire
For what they died; who had the same desire.
But above His declining head they hung   95
A table in three languages: the tongue
The first of tongues, which taught our Abrahamites
Those heav'nly precepts, and mysterious rites;
Next, that which to th' informéd world imparts
The Grecian industry, and learnéd arts;   100
Then this, from whence the conquer'd earth now
    takes
Her laws, and at the Roman virtue quakes;
All of one sense: His place of birth, His name
Declare; and for the Hebrew King proclaim.
After the bloody priests so long had fed   105
On this lov'd spectacle, at length they read
The title: and in such a misery,
So full of ruth, found something to envy:
The governor intreating to take down
That glorious style, lest He the Hebrew crown 110

A TRAGEDY. 471

Should vindicate in death; and so deny
That princes by subordinates should die.
But who that day so readily complied
To give a life, austerely this denied.

CHORUS.

While ling'ring death His sad release deferr'd, 115
How look'd the standers-by? what words were
    heard?

FIRST NUNCIUS.

Not all alike: discording murmurs rise.
Some, with transfixéd hearts, and wounded eyes,
Astonish'd stand; some joy in His slow fate,
And to the last extend their barbarous hate. 120
Motion itself variety begets,
And, by a strange vicissitude, regrets
What it affected, nor one posture bears:
Tears scornful laughter raise, and laughter tears.
Who to the Temple from th' impoverish'd shore 125
Of Galilee His follow'd steps adore,
And minister'd to His life, now of His end
The witnesses, still to their dying Friend
Their faith preserve; which, as they could, they
    show
In all th' expressions of a perfect woe. 130
One, from her panting breast her garments tare;
Another, the bright tresses of her hair;
This, with her naked arms her bosom beats;
The hollow rock her fearful shrieks repeats,
She stiff with sorrow. But what grief could vie 135
With that example of all piety,
His Virgin Mother's! this affords no way
To lessening tears, nor could itself display.
Where should she fix her looks? If on the ground,
She sees that with her blood, He bleeding, drown'd:

Or if she raise her eyes, the killing sight 141
Of her womb's tortur'd Issue quench'd their light.
Fearing to look on either, both disclose
Their terrors; who now licenses her woes.
Ready to have stept forward, and embrac'd 145
The bloody Cross, her feeble limbs stuck fast:
Her feet their motion lost; her voice in vain
A passage sought: such grief could not complain.
Whose soul almost as great a sorrow stung,
As His Who on the tree in torments hung. 150
That youth, one of the twelve, so dignified
By his dear Master's love, stood by her side.
Beholding this sad pair—those souls that were
To Him than life, while life remain'd, more dear—
He found another cross: His spirits melt, 155
More for the sorrow seen than torments felt.
At length, in strength transcending either, brake
The bars of His long silence, and thus spake:
" A legacy to each of you I leave:
Mother, this son instead of Me receive 160
By thy adoption; and, thou gentle boy,
The seed of Zebedeus, late My joy,
Thy friend now for thy mother take." This said,
Again He to His torments bow'd His Head.
The vulgar, with the elders of our race, 165
And soldiers, shake their heads in His disgrace:
" Is this the Man," said they, " Whose Hands can raze
The Temple, and rebuild it in three days ?
Now show Thy strength. Or if the Thunderer
Above the rank of mortals Thee prefer, 170
Acknowledg'd for His Heir, let Him descend,
Confirm Thy hopes, and timely succour lend.
Behold, the help Thou gav'st to others fails
The Author. Break these bonds, these stubborn nails,

And from the Cross descend : then we will say 175
Thou art our King, and Thy commands obey."
Nor was't enough that the surrounding throng
Wound with reproaches : who beside him hung
Doth now again a murderer's mind disclose,
And in his punishment more wicked grows.   180
Who thus : " If thou be He Whom God did choose
To govern the freed nation of the Jews,
Thyself and us release; thus honour win."
The partner of his death, as of his sin,
Who had his fierceness with the thief cast off,   185
Ill brooks, and thus reproves the impious scoff:
" Hast thou as yet not learnt to acknowledge God,
Nor sacred justice fear, who now the rod
Of vengeance feel'st ? wilt thou again offend,
And to the jaws of hell thy guilt extend ?   190
This death we owe to our impiety;
But what are His misdeeds? why should He die?"
Then looking on His Face with drooping eyes,
" Forgive me, O forgive a wretch," He cries,
"And O my Lord, my King, when Thou shalt be 195
Restor'd to Thy own heav'n, remember me."
He mildly gives consent; and from the bars
Of that sad Cross, thus rais'd him to the stars :
" With Me, a happy guest, thou shalt enjoy
Those sacred orchards, where no frosts destroy 200
The eternal spring, before the morn display
The purple ensign of th' ensuing day."

CHORUS.

What's this ! the centre pants with sudden throes !
And trembling earth a sad distemper shows !
The sun, affrighted, hides his golden head,   205
From hence by an unknown ecliptic fled !
Irregular heavens abortive shades display,
And night usurps the empty throne of day !

What threats do these dire prodigies portend
To our offending race? Those ills transcend 210
All that can be imagin'd, which enforce
Disturbéd nature to forget her course.
I hear approaching feet: Whate'er thou art,
Whom darkness from our sight conceals, impart
All that thou know'st to our preparéd ears: 215
Accomplish, or dissolve our pressing fears.

SECOND NUNCIUS.

Fury (from which, if loose, the earth had fled)
And fatal stars have their event: He's dead!

CHORUS.

O heaven! we pardon now day's hasty flight,
Nor will complain, since they have quench'd this
    light. 220
Yet tell how He dispos'd of His last breath,
The passages and order of His death.

SECOND NUNCIUS.

As the declining sun the shades increas'd,
Reflecting on the more removéd east,
His blazing hair grew black; no cloud obscures 225
His vanish'd light; this his own orb immures.
The day's fourth part as yet invests the pole,
Were this a day, when from the Afflicted Soul,
This Voice was clearly heard, not like the breath
Of those who labour between life and death: 230
"My God, O why dost Thou Thy own forsake?"
Which purposely the multitude mistake,
But to prolong their cruel mirth: who said,
He on the Thesbian Prophet[1] calls for aid,
Now to return, and draw from heav'n again 235
Devouring show'rs of fire, or floods of rain.
With silence this He endures. His body rent,
His blood exhausted, and His spirits spent,

---

[1] Elijah the Tishbite.

A TRAGEDY. 475

He cried, "I thirst." As servants to His will,
The greedy hollows of a sponge they fill   240
With vinegar, which hyssop sprigs combine,
And on a reed exalt the deadly wine.
This scarcely tasted, His pale lips once more
He opens, and now louder than before
Cried, "All is finish'd; here My labours end: 245
To Thee, O Heavenly Father, I commend
My parting Soul." This said, hung down His head,
And with. His words His mixéd Spirits fled,
Leaving His Body, which again must bleed,
Now senseless of the Cross. From prison freed, 250
Those happy seats He enjoys, by God assign'd
To injur'd virtue, and th' etherial mind.
But terrors, which with nature war, affright
Our peaceless souls. The world hath lost its Light:
Heav'n, and the deeps below, our guilt pursue: 255
Pale troops of wand'ring ghosts now hurry through
The Holy City; whom from her unknown
And secret womb the trembling earth hath thrown.
The cleaving rocks their horrid jaws display,
And yawning tombs afford the dead a way   260
To those that live. Heaven is the general
And undistinguish'd sepulchre to all.
Old Chaos now returns. Ambitious night,
Impatient of alternate rule, or right,
Such as before the day's etherial birth   265
With her own shady people fills the earth.

Chorus.
How did the many-minded people look,
At these portents? with what affection strook?

Second Nuncius.
The lamentations, mixéd with the cries
Of weeping women, in loud volleys rise.   270

Those who had known Him, who His followers
 were
While yet He liv'd, and did in death adhere,
In that new night sighs from their sorrows send,
And, to those heav'ns they could not see, extend
Their pious hands, complaining that the sun   275
Would then appear when this was to be done.
The safety of their lives the vulgar dread;
Some for themselves lament, some for the dead;
Others the ruin of the world bewail.
Their courages the cruel Romans fail: 280
Those hands, which knew no peace, now lazy grew;
And conqu'ring fear to earth their weapons threw.
Th' amaz'd centurion with our thoughts complied,
And swore the Hero most unjustly died:
Whose punishment the earth could hardly brook,
But groaning, with a horrid motion shook.   286
Confirméd by the day's prodigious flight
To be a beam of the celestial light:
And so the mourning heav'n's inverted face
Shows to the under world His heav'nly race.   290

CHORUS.

Why flock the people to the Temple thus?
No cause, excepting piety, in us
Can want belief. Hope they to satisfy
With sacrifice the wrath of the Most High?

SECOND NUNCIUS.

New prodigies, as horrid, thither hale   295
Th' astonish'd multitude. The Temple's veil,
That hung on gilded beams in purple dy'd,
Asunder rent, and fell on either side.
The trust of what was sacred is betray'd,
And all the Hebrew mysteries display'd.   300
That fatal Ark, so terrible of old
To our pale foes, which cherubims of gold

A TRAGEDY.

Veil'd with their hov'ring wings; whose closure held
Those two-leav'd Tables, wherein God reveal'd
His Sacred Laws; that Food, which by a new   305
Example fell from heav'n in fruitful dew
About our tents, and tacitly express'd
By intermitted show'rs the Seventh Day's rest;
The Rod with never-dying blossoms spread,
Which with a mitre honour Aaron's head: 310
These with th' old Temple perish'd: th' eye could reach
No object in this rupture but the breach.
What was from former ages hid is shown;
Which struck so great a rev'rence when unknown.
The Temple shines with flames; and to the sight 315
That fear'd recess disclos'd with its own light.
Either religion from their fury flies,
Leaving it naked to profaner eyes:
Or God doth this abhorréd seat reject,
And will His Temple in the mind erect.   320

CHORUS.

Shall punishment in death yet find an end?
Shall His cold corpse to earth in peace descend?
Or naked hang, and with so dire a sight
Profane the vesper of the sacred night?

SECOND NUNCIUS.

Too late religion warms their savage breasts,   325
Lest that near hour which harbingers their Feast
Should take them unprepar'd; to Pilate they
Repair; entreat him that the soldier may
From bloody crosses take their bodies down
Before their festivals the morning crown,   330
That no uncleanness might from thence arise,
In memory of th' Egyptian sacrifice.

The legs of the two thieves they break, whose
    breath
Yet groan'd between the bounds of life and death.
The crashing bones report a dreadful sound,   335
While both their souls at once a passage found.
Nor had the cohort less to Jesus done,
Who now the course prescrib'd by fate had run :
But dead, deep in His Side his trembling spear
A soldier strake: His entrails bare appear;   340
And from that wide-mouth'd orifice a flood
Of water gush'd mix'd with a stream of blood.
The Crosses now dischargéd of their fraught,
The people fled; not with one look or thought;
Part sad and part amaz'd. Spent fury dies.   345
Whither so fast? run you to sacrifice
A silly lamb? Too mean an offering
Is this for you, who have sacrific'd your King.

CHORUS.

Either deceiv'd by the ambiguous day,
Or troops of mourners to my eyes display   350
A perfect sorrow: women with their bare
And bleeding breasts, drown'd cheeks, dishevell'd
    hair.
The soldiers slowly march, with knees that bend
Beneath their fears, and Pilate's stairs ascend.

CHORUS OF ROMAN SOLDIERS.

THOU who on thy flaming chariot
    rid'st,   355
And with perpetual motion time divid'st,
Great king of day, from whose far-darting eye
Night-wand'ring stars with fainting splendour
    fly,

A TRAGEDY.

Whither, thus intercepted, dost thou stray?
Through what an unknown darkness lies thy
    way?   360
In heav'n what new-born night the day invades?
The mariner, that sails by Tyrian Gades,
As yet sees not thy panting horses steep
Their fiery fetlocks in th' Hesperian deep.
No pitchy storm, wrapt up in swelling clouds, 365
By earth exhal'd, thy golden tresses shrouds;
Nor thy pale sister in her wand'ring race
With interposéd wheels obscures thy face;
But now far-off retires with her stol'n light,
Till in a silver orb her horns unite.   370
Hath some Thessalian witch with charms unknown
Surpris'd and bound thee? What new Phaeton,
With feeble hands to guide thy chariot strives,
And far from the deserted zodiac drives?
What horrid façt, before th'approach of night, 375
Deservedly deprives the world of light:
As when stern Atreus to his brother gave
His children's flesh, who made his own their
    grave;
Or when the vestal Ilia's god-like son,
Who our unbounded monarchy begun,   380
Was in a hundred pieces cut, by theft
At once of life and funerals bereft?
Or hath that day wherein the gods were born
Finish'd the course of heav'n in its return;
And now the aged stars refuse to run   385
Beyond that place from whence they first begun?
Nature, what plagues dost thou to thine intend?
Whither shrinks this huge mass? what fatal end?
If now the general flood again retire,
If the world perish by licentious fire,   390
What shall of those devouring seas become?
Where shall those funeral ashes find a tomb?

Whatever innovates the course of things,
To men alone, nor nations, ruin brings :
Either the groaning world's disorder'd frame   395
Now suffers, or that pow'r which guides the same.
Do proud Titanians, with their impious war,
Again provoke th' Olympian Thunderer ?
Is there a mischief extant greater than
Dire Python, or the Snake of Lerna's fen,   400
That poisons the pure heav'ns with viperous breath ?
What god, from gods deriv'd, oppress'd by death,
Is now in his own heav'n bewail'd ? Divine
Lyæus gave to man less precious wine ;
Not Hercules so many monsters slew ;   405
Unshorn Apollo less in physic knew.
Sure we with darkness are envelopéd
Because that innocent Blood by envy shed,
So dear unto the gods, this place defam'd,
Which shook the earth, and made the day asham'd.
Great Father of us all, Whose influence   411
Informs the world Thou mad'st, though sin incense
Thy just displeasure, easy to forgive
Those who confess, and for their vices grieve,
Now to the desperate sons of men, who stray   415
In sin's dark labyrinth, restore the day.
One sacrifice seek we to expiate
All our offences, and appease his hate.
Which the religion of the Samian,
Nor Thracian harp, wild beasts instructing, can ;   420
Nor that prophetic boy, the glebe's swart son,
Who taught the Tuscans divination.
The Blood which from that mangled Body bled
Must purge our sins, Which we unjustly shed.
O smooth Thy brows ! Receive the innocence   425
Of One for all ; and with our guilt dispense.
For sin, what greater ransom can we pay ?
What worthier offering on Thy altar lay ?

ANNOTATIONS ON THE FOURTH ACT.

VER. 35. *To war a fatal way.*] The city of Jerusalem is only on that side assailable; there forced and entered by the Babylonians, and after by Pompey.

Ver. 36. *Golgotha.*] Mount Calvary: a rocky hill, neither high nor ample, lying then without the north-west wall of the city: the public place of execution. Here they say that Abraham would have sacrificed Isaac; in memory whereof there now standeth a chapel: as an altar, where the head of Adam was found, which gave the name to that mount; buried in that place where his bones might be sprinkled with the real Blood of our Saviour, which he knew would be there shed by a prophetical foreknowledge. It is said to stand in the midst of the earth; which must needs be meant by the then habitable, for what middle can there be in a spherical body?

Ver. 49. *The Nazarite.*] Not as Samson by vow, nor of that sect; but so called of that city, wherein He was conceived, and where He inhabited after His return out of Egypt.

Ver. 52. *Mixed with the bitter tears of myrrh.*] Some suppose that this was proffered Him by His friends, being of a stupefying quality, to make Him less sensible of His torments. But it appears by Petronius and Pliny that it was a mixture much used in their delights. Whereof Martial :—

"The tears of myrrh in hot Falernum thaw :
From this the wine a better taste will draw."
Epig. l. 14.

Strengthening the body, and refreshing the spirits; and therefore more likely proffered by His enemies to prolong His sufferings.

Ver. 81. *His inward robe.*] There be who write that this was woven by the Virgin Mary; and we read in the Scriptures, as frequently in Homer and other authors, that women, and those of the highest quality, usually wrought garments for their children and husbands.

Ver. 203. *The centre pants, &c.*] This earthquake proceeded not from the winds imprisoned in the bowels of the earth struggling to break forth, or from any other natural cause, but by the immediate Finger of God.

Ver. 205. *The sun, affrighted, hides, &c.*] Miraculous, without the interposition of the moon, or palpable vapours, was that defect of the sun, and unnatural darkness, in the sixth hour of the day; which appeareth by the text to have covered all the world, and not Judea alone, as some have conjectured. Divers authors have recorded this in their annals and histories; but none so exactly as Dionysius Areopagita, who then resided in Egypt, and was an eyewitness.

Ver. 240. *The greedy hollows of a sponge, &c.*] Physicians agree that vinegar being drunk, or held to the nose, hath in it a natural virtue for the stanching of blood. Pliny attributes the like to hyssop, and the better if joined. Neither is it to be thought that the Jews offered this unto Jesus in humanity, but rather out of their hatred; that, by prolonging His life until the evening, His legs might have been broken, to the increase of His torments.

Ver. 256. *Pale troops of wandering ghosts.*] These were the real bodies of the dead, which entered the city from their graves (for it was, as now, their custom to bury in the fields) and seen by day. Whereas deluding spirits assume an airy, thin, and fluxative body, condensed by cold, but dissipated by heat, and therefore only appear in the night-time. Which Virgil intimates in the ghost of Anchises:—

"And now farewell: the humid night descends;
I scent day's breath in his too swift repair.
This said, like smoke he vanisheth to air."

Aen. 1. 5.

Ver. 259. *The cleaving rocks.*] The rock of Mount Calvary was rent by that earthquake from the top to the bottom, which at this day is to be seen: the rupture such as art could have no hand in; each side answerable ragged, and there where unaccessible to the workman.

Ver. 263. *Old chaos now returns.*] That confused mass, out of which God created the beautiful world; into which it was imagined that it should be again reduced:—

"The aged world, dissolvéd by the last
And fatal hour, shall to old Chaos haste.
Stars, justling stars, shall in the deep confound
Their radiant fires: the land shall give no bound
To swallowing seas: the moon shall cross the sun,
With scorn that her swift wheels obliquely run,
Day's throne aspiring. Discord then shall rend
The world's crack'd frame, and nature's concord end."
Lucan. l. 4.

But many of our divines are of opinion that the world shall neither be dissolved nor annihilated; strengthening their assertion out of the eighth of the Romans, and other places of Scripture.

Ver. 283. *The amaz'd centurion.*] To this centurion, who professed Christ to be the Son of God, they give the name of Longinus, and honour him with the crown of martyrdom.

Ver. 296. *The Temple's veil.*] Described by Josephus to consist of violet, purple, and scarlet silk, cunningly mixed and wrought by Babylonian needles; the colours containing a mystical sense. Such was that of Solomon's, and of the travelling tabernacle, but that they were powdered with cherubims. This, it should seem, was renewed by Herod when he so magnificently repaired the Temple. It hung before the Sanctum Sanctorum, into which none but the high priest, and that but once in the year, was to enter; violated by Pompey, pursued by a miserable destiny. There was an outward veil, not unlike the other, which separated the priests from the people: this, contrary to the opinion of our author, Baronius conceives to be that which then rent asunder; interpreted to signify the final abolishing of the Law Ceremonial. They write that at the tearing thereof a dove was seen to fly out of the Temple.

Ver. 319. *Or God doth this abhorr'd, &c.*] Eusebius, St. Jerome, and others report, that with this earthquake at the Passion, the doors of the Temple flew open, and that the tutelar angels were heard to cry, "Let us remove from this place;" though Josephus refers it to the destruction of the Temple.

Ver. 362. *Tyrian Gades.*] Gades, now called Cales, an island lying on the South of Spain without Hercules Pillars, held to be the uttermost confines of the Western world, was planted by a colony of the Tyrians.

Ver. 363. *As yet sees not thy panting horses, &c.*] A chariot and horses were attributed to the sun, in regard to the swiftness of his motion; and to express what is beyond the object of the sense by that which is subject unto it. These also by the idolatrous Jews were consecrated unto him. The sun was feigned to descend into the sea, because it so appeareth to the eye; the horizon being there most conspicuous.

Ver. 371. *Hath some Thessalian witch, &c.*] The Thessalian women were infamous for their enchantments; said to have the power to darken the sun, and draw the moon from her sphere. Such Lucan's Erictho:—

"Her words to poison the bright moon aspire;
First pale, then red, with dark and terrene fire:
As when deprived of her brother's sight,
Earth interposing his celestial light:
Perplex'd with tedious charms, and held below,
Till she on under herbs her jelly throw."

Phar. l. 6.

The author of this opinion was Aglonice, the daughter of Hegæmon; who, being skilful in astronomy, boasted to the Thessalian women (foreknowing the time of her eclipse) that she would perform it at such a season, which happening accordingly; and they beholding the distempered moon, gave credit to her deception. The like may arise from the eclipses of the sun.

Ver. 372. *What new Phaeton.*] The fable of Phaeton, the son of Phœbus, as the allegory, is notorious; who, by misguiding the chariot of the sun set all the world on a conflagration.

Ver. 377. *As when stern Atreus, &c.*] Atreus, having

had his bed dishonoured by his brother Thyestes, slew his children, and gave them for food to their father; when the sun, to avoid so horrid a sight, fled back to the Orient. So feigned in that Atreus first discovered the annual course of the sun, which is contrary to his diurnal.

Ver. 379. *Ilia's god-like son, &c.*] Romulus, cut into a hundred pieces by the hundred lords of the senate for being so rigorous to them, and so indulgent to the people; every one carrying a piece away with him under his long gown to conceal the murder: when Julius Proculus, to appease the people, swore that he saw him ascend into heaven, whereupon they consecrated temples unto him, and gave him divine honours; changing his name into Quirinus.

Ver. 383. *Or hath that day, &c.*] The Great Year; when all the planets (here called gods because they carry their names) shall return to that position which they were in at the beginning, comprising, according to Cicero's *Hortensius*, the revolution of twelve thousand nine hundred and fifty years.

Ver. 390. *If the world perish by licentious fire.*] The Romans could not then have this from St. Peter, but rather from the prophecies of the Sibyls :—

"These signs the world's combustion shall fore-run;
Arms clashing, trumpets, from the rising sun
Horrible fragors, heard by all: this frame
Of nature then shall feed the greedy flame.
Men, cities, floods, and seas, by rav'nous lust
Of fire devour'd, all shall resolve to dust."
Orac. l. 4.

From hence, perhaps, the ancient philosophers derived their opinions, as Seneca a latter :—The stars shall encounter one another, and what now shines so orderly shall burn in one fire.

Ver. 395. *Either the groaning world, &c.*

Ver. 397. *Do proud Titanians, &c.*] The poets feign that the angry earth, to be revenged of the gods, brought forth the Titans, as after the giants; who, by throwing mountains upon mountains, attempted to scale the heavens and disenthrone Jupiter, who overthrew them with his lightning and cast those congested mountains upon them.

Pherecydes the Syrian writes, how the devils were cast out of heaven by Jupiter (this fall of the giants perhaps alluding to that of the angels) the chief called Ophionius, which signifies serpentine, having after made use of that creature to poison Eve with a false ambition.

Ver. 400. *Dire Python.*] A prodigious serpent, which after Deucalion's flood lay upon the earth like a mountain, and slain by Apollo; the sense of the fable being merely physical. For Python, born after the deluge of the humid earth, was that great exhalation which rose from the late drowned world, at length dissipated by the fervour of the sun, or Apollo :—

"The earth then soak'd in showers, yet, hardly dry,
Threw up thick clouds, which darken'd all the sky:
This was that Python."—*Pont. Meteor.*

The word signifies putrefaction; and because the sun consumes the putrefaction of earth, his beams darting from his orb like arrows, with his arrows he is said to have slain Python.

Ver. 400. *Lerna's Fen.*] In this lay that venomous serpent Hydra, which is said to have many heads, whereof one being cut off two rose in the room, more terrible than the former, and with her poisonous breath to have infected all the territories adjoining. This fable had a relation to that place which through the eruption of waters annoyed the neighbouring cities, when one being stopped many rose in the room; this Hercules perceiving, burnt them with fire :—

"Corruption boils away with heat;
And forth superfluous vapours sweat."

But physically Hydra signifies water; and Hercules, according to Macrobius, presenteth the sun, whose extraordinary fervour dried up those noisome and infectious vapours.

Ver. 404. *Lyæus gave to man less precious wine.*] Lyæus is a name of Bacchus, because wine refresheth the heart and freeth it from sorrow. Noah was he who immediately after the Flood first planted a vineyard, and showed the use of wine unto man ; wherefore some write that of Noachus he was called Boachus, and after Bacchus by the Ethnicks, either by contraction or through ignorance of the etymology. This comparison hath relation to Christ's conversion of water into such excellent wine at Cana in Galilee.

Ver. 405. *Not Hercules so many monsters slew.*] Hercules, saith Seneca, travelled over the world, not to oppress it, but to free it from oppressors, and by killing of tyrants and monsters to preserve it in tranquillity. But how much more glorious were the victories of Christ, Who by suffering for sin subdued it, led captivity captive, was the death of Death, triumphing over hell and those spirits of darkness.

Ver. 406. *Unshorn Apollo less in physic knew.*] Apollo, to whom they attribute long yellow hair in regard of his beautiful beams, is said to have invented the art of physic (his name importing a preservation from evil) because the sun is so powerful in producing physical simples, and so salubrious to our bodies: when Christ by His own virtue cured all diseases; gave sight to the blind by birth, which surpasseth the power of art; threw out wicked spirits from the tortured bodies of the possessed; and called the dead from their beds of death to converse again with the living.

Ver. 419. *Which the religion of the Samian.*] Of Pythagoras of Samos; who, by his doctrine and example, withdrew the Crotonians from luxury and idleness to temperance and industry; calming the perturbations of the mind with the music of his harp, for he held that virtue, strength, all good, and even God Himself, consisted of harmony: that God was the soul of the world, from whence each creature received his life, and, dying, restored it. And, lest it might be doubted that the souls of all had not one original, in regard of their different understandings, he alleged how that proceeded from the natural complexion and composition of the body, as more or less perfect, whose opinions are thus delivered by Virgil:—

"The archéd heavens, round earth, the liquid plain,
The moon's bright orb, and stars Titanian,
A soul within sustains; whose virtues pass
Through every part, and mix with that huge mass :
Hence men, hence beasts, whatever fly with wing,
And monsters in the marble ocean spring :
Of seed divine, and fiery vigour, full,
But what gross flesh and dying member dull.
Thence fear, desire, grief, joy, nor more regard
Their heavenly birth, in those blind prisons barr'd."
Æn. l. 6.

Moreover, he held that this visible soul or godhead, diffused throughout all the world, got itself such diversity of names by the manifold operations which it effected in every part of the visible universe.

Ver. 420. *Nor Thracian harp, wild beasts instructing, can.*] Orpheus of Thrace, who, with the music of his harp and voice attracted even beasts and senseless stones to hear him. The moral of which fable may parallel with that of Amphion:—

"Orpheus, the gods' interpreter, from blood
Rude men at first deterr'd, and savage food :
Hence said to have tigers and fell lions tamed.
Amphion so, who Theban bulwarks framed,
T' have led the stones with music of his lute
And mild requests. Of old in high repute :
Public from private, sacred from profane
To separate ; and wandering lust restrain
With matrimonial ties; fair cities raise;
Laws stamp in brass. This gave the honour'd bays
To sacred poets, and to verse their praise."
Horat. de Art. Poet.

It is apparent, by his testament to his scholar Musæus (whereof certain verses are recited by Justin Martyr) that his opinion in divinity was, in the main, agreeable with the Sacred Scriptures. As of one God, the Creator of heaven and earth, the Author of all good, and Punisher of all evil; exhorting him to the hearing and understanding of that knowledge which was revealed from Heaven; meaning nothing else by those various names which he gives to the gods, but divine and natural virtues; shadowing God Himself, under the name of Jupiter, to avoid the envy and danger of those times, as is almost evident by these attributes.

"Omnipotent Jove ; the first, the last of things;
The head, the midst; all from Jove's bounty springs.
Foundation of the earth and starry sky ;
A male, a female, who can never die.
Spirit of all, the force of awful fire ;
Source of the sea, sun, moon, the original,
The end of all things, and the king of all.
At first conceal'd; then, by His wondrous might
And sacred goodness, all produc'd to light."

Ver. 421. *Nor that prophetic boy*, &c.] Of whom Ovid :—

"The nymphs and Amazonian this amaz'd,
No less than when the Tyrrhene ploughman gaz'd
Upon the fatal clod that mov'd alone;
And for a human shape exchang'd his own.
With infant lips, that were but earth of late,
Reveal'd the mysteries of future fate;
Whom natives Tages call'd. He, first of all,
Th' Hetrurians taught to tell what would befall."
Met. l. 15.

And Cicero, in his second book of Divination : "Tages, when the earth was turned up and the plough had made a deeper impression, ascended (as they say) in the Tarquinian fields, and spake to the tiller. It is written in the Hetrurian Records that he was seen in the form of a boy, although old in wisdom. The husbandman, amazed and exalting his voice, drew thither a great concourse of people, and within awhile all Tuscany; who spake many things in that populous audience, by them remembered and committed to writing. His oration only contained the discipline of divination by the entrails of beasts, which after increased by experience, but is referred to this original. A delusion of the devil's to introduce that superstition."

THE FIFTH ACT.

JOSEPH OF ARIMATHEA. NICODEMUS.

EE, citizens, we Pilate's bounty bear:
Without a suit men cannot man inter.
The Roman progeny nor freely will
Do what is good; nor, unrewarded, ill.
Nothing is now in use but barbarous vice: 5
They sell our blood, on graves they set a price.

NICODEMUS.

O Joseph, these vain ecstasies refrain!
But if it seem so pleasant to complain,
Let Rome alone, and seek a nearer guilt:
His Blood not Romulus' sons, but Abraham's,
    spilt.   10
Whoso the purer sense sincerely draws
From those Celestial Oracles and Laws,
By God above Himself inspir'd, will say,
None led to eternity a straighter way.
What's that to Pilate? fell the Innocent by   15
A Roman oath? was't through the subtilty
Of senators or priests? The doom display'd,
They Cæsar less than Caiaphas obey'd.
Let us transfer the fact: the impious Jew
With heart, with tongue and eyes, first Jesus
    slew: 20

The Romans only acted their offence.
How well the heavens with Hebrew hands dispense!
For this the Jew th' Italian's crime envied,
And wish'd himself the bloody homicide.
Do we as yet our servitude lament,   25
When such a murder meets no punishment?
This do they, this command.

JOSEPH.

                          The progeny
Of Roman Ilia and of Sara I
With equal detestation execrate :
O may they perish by a fearful fate!   30
Just Heaven, why sleeps thy lightning? In a
  show'r
Of pitch descend : Let stanching seas devour
This cursed city! Sodom, thou art clear,
Compared to ours. No more will I a tear
Shed for my country. Let the Great in war,   35
Worse than the Babylonian conqueror,
Enter her breaches like a violent flood,
Until the bloody city swim in blood.
Is this too little? Let diseases sow
Their fruitful seed, and in destruction grow :   40
Famine, in their dry entrails take thy seat;
What nature most abhors, enforce to eat.
Let th' infant tremble at his father's knife ;
The babe re-enter her who gave it life.
While yet the eager foe invests the wall,   45
Within may they by their own weapons fall :
The Temple wrapt in flames. Let th' enemy
Decide their civil discord, and destroy
With fire and sword ungrateful Solyma :
The relics of their slaughter drive away ;   50
Nor seventy years dissolve their servile bands ;
Despis'd and wretched, wander through all lands :

Abolish'd be their law, all form of state;
No day see their return. Let sudden fate
Succeed my curses. This infected soil 55
No more shall feed me. What unusual toil
Shall my old feet refuse, so they no more
Tread on this earth! though to that unknown shore,
Which lies beneath the slow Boötes' wain,
Dash'd by th' inconstant billows of that main. 60
That country shall be mine where justice sways,
And bold integrity the truth obeys.

NICODEMUS.
This error with a secret poison feeds
The mind's disease. Who censures his own deeds?
Who not another's? These accusing times 65
Rather the men condemn than tax their crimes.
Such is the tyranny of judgment; prone
To sentence all offences but our own.
Because of late we cried not "Crucify,"
Nor falsely doom'd the Innocent to die, 70
Ourselves we please, as it a virtue were,
And great one, if from great offences clear.
Confess; what orator would plead His cause?
To vindicate His truth who urg'd the laws?
Or once accus'd their bloody suffrages, 75
By envy sign'd? Who durst those lords displease?
So piety suffer'd, while by speaking they,
And we by silence, did the Just betray.
When women openly their zeal durst show,
We, in acknowledging our Master, slow, 80
Under the shady coverture of night
Secur'd our fears, which would not brook the light.
Joseph, at length, our faith itself exprest:
But to the dead.

A TRAGEDY.

JOSEPH.
This is a truth confess'd.
The evening now restoréd day subdues: 85
And lo, the vigil with the night ensues.
Not far from Golgotha's infamous rocks
A cave there is, hid with the shady locks
Of funeral cypress, hewn through living stone:
The house of death; as yet possess'd by none. 90
My age this chose for her eternal rest;
Which now shall entertain a nobler Guest.
That ample stone, which shuts the sepulchre,
Shall the inscription of His virtues bear.
Who knows but soon a holier age may come, 95
When all the world shall celebrate this tomb,
And kings, as in a temple, here adore,
Through fire and sword sought from the farthest
    shore?

NICODEMUS.
Pure water of the spring, you precious tears!
Perfumes which odour-breathing Saba bears, 100
With your preservatives His Body lave,
Sink through His pores, and from corruption save.
Nor God nor fate will suffer, that this Pure,
This Sacred Corpse should more than death endure.
Religion, if thou know'st the shades below, 105
Let never filthy putrefaction flow
Through His uncover'd bones; nor waste of time
Resolve this Heavenly Figure into slime.

JOHN.   MARY THE MOTHER OF JESUS.

THOU rev'rend Virgin, of his royal blood,
Who all between the Erythrean flood
And great Euphrates won by strenuous
    arms, 111
Assume his noble fortitude: those harms

Which press thy soul subdue: ungentle Fate
Hath by undoing thee secur'd thy state.
Fortune her strength by her own blows hath spent.
Judæa's kingdom from thy fathers rent 116
By foreign hands: of ancient wealth bereft,
Except thy Son; what was for danger left?
These storms, by death dispers'd, serene appear;
For what hath childless poverty to fear? 120

MARY.

O John, for thee in such extremes to mourn
Perhaps is new; but I to grief was born.
With this have we convers'd twice-sixteen years;
No form of sorrow hath beguiled our fears.
To me how ominously the prophets sung, 125
Ev'n from the time that Heav'nly Infant sprung
In my chaste womb! Old Simeon this reveal'd,
And in my soul the deadly wound beheld.
When One, among so many infants slain,
Was by the tyrant's weapons sought in vain, 130
No miracles had then His fame display'd,
Or Him the object of their envy made.
Perfidious fraud in sanctity's disguise,
Nor the adulterated Pharisees,
By His detection had He yet inflam'd; 135
Nor for despising of their rites defam'd:
A trumpet of intestine war: the earth
Of nothing then accus'd Him, but His birth.
Not that fierce prince, so cruel to his own;
Nor his successor in that fatal throne, 140
As high in vice, who with the prophet's head
Supplied his feast, and on the blood he had shed
Fed his incestuous eyes, in dire delight
To heighten impious love, could me affright:
Nor yet the vulgar, hating His free tongue; 145
And show'rs of stones by a thousand furies flung.

I thought no mischief could our steps pursue,
That was more great, or to our suff'rings new.
What wants example, what no mother feared,
This, this alone my dying hopes interr'd. 150
Wretch, wilt thou seek for words t' express thy
   woes?
Or this so vast a grief in silence close?
Great God (such is my faith) why would'st Thou
   come
To this inferior kingdom through my womb?
Why mad'st Thou choice of me to bring Thee forth
For punishment? unhappy in my worth! 156
No woman ever bare a son, by touch
Of man conceiv'd, whose soul endures so much:
No mother such an issue better gain'd,
Nor lost it worse; by cursèd death profan'd. 160

JOHN.

What louder grief with such an emphasis
Strikes through mine ears? What honour'd Corse
   is this,
With Tyrian linen veil'd? What's he whose hairs
Contend with snow, whose eyes look through their
   tears;
Who on those veins, yet bleeding, odours pours?
Or his assistant, crown'd with equal hours? 166
What troops of women hither throng! what storms
Rise in their looks! Grief wanders through all
   forms.
My eyes, ah! wound my heart. This was thy Son:
This is thy blood, thy mangled flesh. O run, 170
Take thy last kisses, ere of those bereft
By funeral: what else of all is left?

MARY.

My soul, tired with long misery,
Amidst these greater sorrows die;

While grief at His sad exsequies 175
Pours out her last complaints in these.
Let me this snowy pall unfold,
Once more those quick'ning looks behold.
O Son, born to a sad event,
Thus, thus, to Thy poor mother sent! 180
O Salem, was thy hatred such,
To murder Him Who lov'd so much?
Ah, see His side gor'd with a spear!
Those Hands, that late so bounteous were,
Transfix'd! His Feet pierc'd with one wound! 185
The sun had better never found
His loss, than with restoréd light
To show the world so dire a sight.
You neighbours to the sun's uprise,
Who read their motions in the skies, 190
O you in chief who found your Lord,
And with such lively zeal ador'd,
Now view the heaven's inverted laws;
With me bewail the wretched cause.
His Birth a star, new-kindled, sign'd: 195
To see His Death the sun grew blind.
Thou hope of my afflicted state,
Thou living, I accus'd not fate:
The day again with light is crown'd,
But Thou in night for ever drown'd. 200
O could'st Thou see my broken heart!
The flowing tears these springs impart!
Thy mother, whom man never knew,
Who by the Word then fruitful grew:
My womb admir'd that unknown Guest, 205
Whose burden for nine moons increas'd.
Thy mother, to a sceptre born,
With age and wrinkling sorrow worn,
This country sees, to get her bread
With labour, in an humble shed. 210

A TRAGEDY.

Thy milk from these two fountains sprung,
These arms about my neck have hung,
Couch'd on the flow'ry banks of Nile:
Egypt, so just to Thy exile,
Hath now redeem'd her former curse; 215
Our Jews than those of Memphis worse.
If His chaste Blood at length assuage
The bitter tempest of your rage;
If you can pity misery,
O let me by your mercy die; 220
Or, if not glutted with His Blood,
With mine increase this purple flood.
O my dear Son! what here our eyes behold,
What yonder hung, or what death could enfold
In endless night, is mine, and only mine; 225
No mortal did in Thy conception join,
Nor part of Thee can challenge: since the loss
Was only ours, let us the grief engross.
Ungrateful man! who his Protector slew, 229
Nor feels his curse, nor then his blessing knew.
Poor Wretch! no soul in Thy defence durst rise:[1]
And now the Murder'd unrevengéd lies.
The lame, who by Thy pow'rful charms were
    made
Sound and swift-footed, ran not to Thy aid:
Those eyes, which never saw the glorious light 235
Before Thy sov'reign touch, avoid Thy sight;
And others, from death's silent mansion by
Thy virtue ravish'd, suffer'd Thee to die.

JOHN.

Too true is thy complaint, too just thy woes;
Such were His friends, whom from a world He
    chose. 240

---

[1] Poor Wretch! simply, *unhappy one; destitute of aid.* The Latin is *inops.*

K K

O desperate faith! from whence, from Whom are we
Thus fallen? our souls from no defection free!
Some sold, forswore Him; none from tainture clear;
All from Him fled to follow their own fear.
Thou Oracle! a Father in Thy care, 245
In love a Brother, the delinquent spare,
In Thy divine affection, O too blest!
Whom yesternight saw leaning on Thy breast:
If love in death survive, if yet as great,
Ev'n by that love Thy pardon I entreat; 250
By this Thy weeping mother: I the heir
By Thee adopted to Thy filial care,
Though alike wretched, and as comfortless,
Yet, as I can, will comfort her distress.
O Virgin-Mother, favour thy relief; 255
Though just, yet moderate thy flowing grief:
Thy down-cast mind by thy own virtue raise:
Th' old prophets fill their volumes with thy praise:
No age but shall through all the round of earth
Sing of that Heavenly Love and Sacred Birth. 260
What female glory parallels thy worth!
So grew a mother, such a Son brought forth!
She who prov'd fruitful in the extreme of age,
And found the truth of that despis'd presage;
She, whose sweet babe, expos'd among the reeds,
Which ancient Nilus with his moisture feeds, 266
Who then, a smiling infant, overcame
The threat'ning flood; aspir'd not to thy fame.
But these expressions are for thee too low;
The opening heav'ns did their observance show: 270
Those radiant troops, which darkness put to flight,
Thy throes assisted in that festive night;
Who over thy adoréd Infant hung
With golden wings, and Alleluiahs sung;
While the old sky, to imitate that Birth, 275
Bare a new star to amaze the wond'ring earth.

MARY.

Sorrow is fled: joy, a long banish'd guest,
With heav'nly rapture fills my enlargéd breast;
More great than that in youth, when from the sky
An angel brought that blesséd embassy; 280
When shame, not soon instructed, blush'd for fear,
How I a Son by such a fate should bear.
I greater things foresee: my eyes behold
Whatever is by destiny enroll'd.
With troops of pious souls, more great than they,
Thou to felicity shalt lead the way. 286
A holy people shall obey Thy throne,
And heav'n itself surrender Thee Thy own.
Subjected death Thy triumph now attends,
While Thou from Thy demolish'd tomb ascends.
Nor shalt Thou long be seen by mortal eyes, 291
But in perfection mount above the skies;
Propitious ever, from that height shalt give
Peace to the world, instructed how to live.
A thousand languages shall Thee adore: 295
Thy empire know no bounds. The farthest shore,
Wash'd by the ocean, those who day's bright flame
Scarce warms, shall hear the thunder of Thy Name.
Licentious sword nor hostile fury shall
Prevail against Thee; Thou, the Lord of all. 300
Those tyrants, whom the vanquish'd worlds obey,
Before Thy feet shall Cæsar's sceptre lay.
The time draws on in which itself must end,
When Thou shalt in a throne of clouds descend
To judge the earth. In that reforméd world, 305
Those by their sins infected, shall be hurl'd
Down under one perpetual night; while they,
Whom Thou hast cleans'd, enjoy perpetual day.

THE END.

ANNOTATIONS ON THE FIFTH ACT.

ERSE 30. *O may they perish, &c.*] This imprecation comprehends those following calamities which the Divine vengeance inflicted on the Jews; more and more horrid than ever befell any other nation.

Ver. 35. *Let the Great in war, &c.*] Titus Vespasian, who besieged Jerusalem when almost all the Jewish nation was within the walls, there met to celebrate the Passover; who took it by force, consumed the Temple with fire (which fell on that day in which it was formerly burnt by the Chaldeans) and levelled the city with the ground; eleven hundred thousand Jews there perishing by famine, pestilence, and the sword; another hundred thousand captives were publicly sold, for a Roman penny a Jew, and sixteen thousand sent to Alexandria for servile employments; two thousand of the most beautiful and personable young men reserved to attend on his triumph, who after, to delight the spectators, were torn in pieces by wild beasts in the amphitheatre.

Ver. 39. *Let diseases sow, &c.*] During the siege the pestilence violently raged, proceeding from the stench of dead bodies, to whom they afforded no burial, but piled them up in their houses, or threw them over the wall of the city.

Ver. 41. *Famine, in their dry entrails, &c.*] Unexpressible was the famine they endured, and pitiful, if they themselves had had any pity; enforced to seeth their girdles and shoes, and fighting fiercely with one another

ANNOTATIONS. 501

for so coarse a diet. Driven in the end to that exigent that they were fain to rake the sinks and privies, and to feed on that which was loathsome to behold; neither could they keep what they found from the rapine of others.

Ver. 44. *The babe re-enter her, &c.*] Hunger had so overcome nature, that a woman of riches and honour, named Mary, being daily robbed of her provision by the seditious, slew her own child which sucked at her breast, and, having soddened one half thereof, eat it; when at the scent of flesh they broke in upon her, who presented them with the rest; the thieves then hardly refraining, though they trembled at so horrid a spectacle.

Ver. 45. *While yet the eager foe, &c.*] The enemy assailed them without, and the seditious massacred one another within; divided into three parties—the zealous, the Idumæan robbers, and the rest of the mutinous citizens: but upon every assault of the Romans, setting their private hatred aside, united themselves as if of one mind, and with admirable courage repulsed the enemy; but upon the least cessation renewed their bloody discord, some beginning with their own hands to set the Temple on fire.

Ver. 47. *Let the enemy, &c.*] See the notes upon the 35th verse.

Ver. 50. *The relics of their slaughter.*] In the days of Adrian the Jews raised a new commotion, of whom his lieutenant, Julius Severus, slew five hundred and fourscore thousand, transporting the rest into Spain by the command of the emperor; so that Jewry was then without Jews, as it continues to this present.

Ver. 52. *Despised and wretched, wander, &c.*] Out of Spain they were banished in the year 1500 by Ferdinand and Emanuel. Now scattered throughout the whole world, and hated by those among whom they live, yet suffered as a necessary mischief; subject to all wrongs and contumelies, who can patiently submit themselves to the times, and to whatsoever may advance their profit.

Ver. 53. *Abolished by their law, &c.*] This they lost in the destruction of their city, yet daily expect that Messias Who is already come; and, as they believe, shall restore them to their temporal kingdom.

Ver. 55. *This infected soil, &c.*] The ecclesiastical

histories report how Joseph of Arimathea, after he had suffered imprisonment by the envy of the Jews, and was delivered by an angel, left his country, and sailed to Marseilles in France; from thence passing over into this island, he preached the Gospel to the Britains and Scots; who there exchanged this life for a better.

Ver. 95. *Who knows but soon a holier age, &c.*] Helena, the mother of Constantine, throwing down the fane of Venus which Adrian had erected on Calvary, covered both the mount and sepulchre with a magnificent temple, which yet hath resisted the injuries of insolence and time; and what was before without, in reverence to the place, is now in the heart of the city. To recover this from the Saracens, divers of the western princes have unfortunately ventured their persons and people; though Godfrey of Boullein, with an army of three hundred thousand, made of the city and country an absolute conquest; whose successors held it for fourscore and nine years, and then beaten out by Saladin the Egyptian sultan. Yet yearly is the sepulchre visited, though now in possession of the Turk, from all parts of the world by thousands of Christians, who there pay their vows and exercise their devotions.

Ver. 109. *Of his royal blood, &c.*] Of David's: see the notes upon the 264th verse of the second act.

Ver. 139. *Not that fierce prince, &c.*] Herod the Great, the Murderer of the Infants; who put three of his sons to death, with his wife Mariamne, whom he franticly affected.

Ver. 140. *Nor his successor, &c.*] Herod Antipas, who cut off the head of John the Baptist.

Ver. 189. *You neighbours to the sun's up-rise.*] The Persian Magi.

FINIS.

APPENDIX.

The following two poems are prefixed to Sandys' translation of "*Ovid's Metamorphoses*" (folio, Oxford, 1632). As they are among the very few specimens of his original compositions, they have been printed here. They are addressed to King Charles I. and his Queen, Henrietta Maria.

APPENDIX.

A PANEGYRIC TO THE KING.

Materiæ respondet Musa.

LOVE, whose transcendent arts the
    poets sing,
By men made more than man, is found
    a king:
Whose thunder and inevitable flame
His justice and majestic awe proclaim:
His cheerful influence and refreshing show'rs,   5
Mercy and bounty, marks of heav'nly pow'rs.
These, free from Jove's disorders, bless thy reign,
And might restore the Golden Age again,
If all men, by thy great example led,
Would that preparéd way to virtue tread.   10
Rare cures, deep prophecies, harmonious lays,
Inspir'd Apollo, crown'd with wisdom's rays.
Thy only touch can heal: Thou to thy state
The better genius, oracle, and fate:
The poet's theme and patron, who at will   15
Canst add t' Augustus' sceptre Maro's quill.
Our world's clear eye, thy Cynthia, ever bright,
When nearest thee displays her fairest light.

May her exalted rays for ever join
In a benevolent aspéct with thine!   20
Not Cupid's wild-fires, but those beams which
   dart
From Venus' purer sphere, inflame thy heart.
Minerva's olive prospers in thy land,
And Neptune's ocean stoops to thy command.
Like Bacchus thy fresh youth and free delights, 25
Not as disguiséd in his frantic rites:
Such as, when he with Phœbus takes his seat
On sacred Nisa, and with quick'ning heat
Inspires the Muses. Thou, our Mercury,
From shades infernal wretches, doom'd to die, 30
Restor'st to light; thy prudent snakes assuage
Hell-nourish'd discord, and war's bloody rage.
Thy zeal to many Mercuries gives wing,
Who heav'nly embassies to mortals bring.
Thy vigilance secure repose imparts,   35
Yet build'st no counsels on his subtle arts.
Those old heroës with their heroines,
Who spangled all the firmament with signs,
Shut out succeeding worthies; scarce could spare
A little room for Berenice's hair.   40
Great Julius, who their gods transcended far,
Could rise no higher than a blazing star.
Others, whom after-ages most admire,
At comets catch, or stars new set on fire;
Which, though etherial, see not their event, 45
So soon, like sublunary glories, spent!
These, whose aspécts gave laws to destiny,
Before the lustre of the day-star fly;
Their lights prov'd erring fires, their influence
   vain,
And nothing but their empty names remain. 50
Those last immortaliz'd, whose dying breath
Pronounced them men, created gods by death;

TO THE KING.

Whom fragrant flames, Jove's eagles, perjuries,
And popular applause, rais'd to the skies;
Down shot like falling stars; more transitory   55
In their divine than in their human glory.
These, as the first, bold flattery deified:
Thou, to whom Heav'n that title hath applied,
Shalt by humility, a grace unknown
To their ambition, gain a heav'nly throne.   60
Enough, my muse! Time shall a poet raise,
Born under better stars, to sing his praise.

URANIA TO THE QUEEN.

HE Muses, by your favour blest,
Fair Queen, invite you to their feast.
The Graces will rejoice, and sue,
Since so excell'd, to wait on you.
Ambrosia taste, which frees from death; 5
And nectar, fragrant as your breath,
By Hebe fill'd; who states the prime
Of youth, and brails the wings of Time.
Here in Adonis' gardens grow
What neither age nor winter know. 10
The Boy, with whom Love seem'd to die,
Bleeds in this pale Anemony.
Self-lov'd Narcissus in the mirror
Of your fair eyes now sees his error,
And from the flattering fountain turns. 15
The Hyacinth no longer mourns.
This Heliotrope, which did pursue
Th' adoréd Sun, converts to you.
These statues touch, and they again
Will from cold marble change to men. 20
Chaste Daphne bends her virgin boughs,
And twines to embrace your sacred brows.
Their tops the Paphian Myrtles move,
Saluting you their Queen of Love.
Myrrha, who weeps for her offence, 25
Presents her tears; her frankincense

Leucothoë; the Heliades
Their amber: yet you need not these.
They all retain their sense, and throng
To hear the Thracian poet's song. 30
How would they, should you sing, admire!
Neglect his skill, as he his lyre!
Contending nightingales, struck mute,
Drop down, and die upon your lute!
The Phœnix, from the glowing East, 35
With sweets here builds her tomb and nest:
Another Phœnix seen, she dies,
Burnt into ashes by your eyes!
This Swan, which in Penëus swims,
His funeral songs converts to hymns. 40
These azure-plum'd Halcyones,
Whose birth controls the raging seas,
To your sweet union yield the praise
Of nuptial loves, of peaceful days.
Nymph, take this quiver and this bow, 45
Diana such in shape and show,
When with her star-like train she crowns
Eurotas' banks or Cynthus' downs.
There chase the Calydonian Boar:
Here see Actæon fly before 50
His eager Hounds. Wild herds will stand
At gaze, nor fear so fair a hand.
There be who our delights despise,
As shadows and vain phantasies.
Those sons of earth, inthrall'd to sense, 55
Condemn what is our excellence.
The air, immortal souls, the skies,
The angels in their hierarchies,
Unseen, to all things seen dispense
Bread, life, protection, influence. 60
Our high conceptions crave a mind
From earth and ignorance refin'd;

Crown virtue; fortune's pride control;
Raise objects equal to the soul:
At will create; eternity 65
Bestow on mortals born to die.
Yet we, who life to others give,
Fair Queen, would by your favour live.

FINIS.

PRINTED BY WHITTINGHAM AND WILKINS,
TOOKS COURT, CHANCERY LANE.

www.ingramcontent.com/pod-product-compliance
Lightning Source LLC
Chambersburg PA
CBHW030015240426
43672CB00007B/954